WINTER
EXPRESS

Easy & delicious **COMFORT FOOD** *ready in a flash*

PUBLISHED IN 2016 BY BOUNTY BOOKS BASED ON MATERIALS LICENSED TO IT BY BAUER MEDIA BOOKS, AUSTRALIA.

BAUER MEDIA BOOKS ARE PUBLISHED BY
BAUER MEDIA PTY LIMITED
54 PARK ST, SYDNEY; GPO BOX 4088,
SYDNEY, NSW 2001 AUSTRALIA
PHONE +61 2 9282 8618; FAX +61 2 9126 3702
WWW.AWWCOOKBOOKS.COM.AU

PUBLISHER
JO RUNCIMAN

EDITORIAL & FOOD DIRECTOR
PAMELA CLARK

DIRECTOR OF SALES, MARKETING & RIGHTS
BRIAN CEARNES

ART DIRECTOR
HANNAH BLACKMORE

SENIOR EDITOR
STEPHANIE KISTNER

JUNIOR EDITOR
AMANDA LEES

FOOD EDITOR
REBECCA MELI

OPERATIONS MANAGER
DAVID SCOTTO

PRINTED IN CHINA
BY LEO PAPER PRODUCTS LTD

PUBLISHED AND DISTRIBUTED IN THE
UNITED KINGDOM BY BOUNTY BOOKS,
A DIVISION OF OCTOPUS PUBLISHING GROUP LTD
CARMELITE HOUSE
50 VICTORIA EMBANKMENT
LONDON, EC4Y 0DZ
UNITED KINGDOM
INFO@OCTOPUS-PUBLISHING.CO.UK;
WWW.OCTOPUSBOOKS.CO.UK

INTERNATIONAL FOREIGN LANGUAGE RIGHTS
BRIAN CEARNES, BAUER MEDIA BOOKS
BCEARNES@BAUER-MEDIA.COM.AU

A CATALOGUE RECORD FOR THIS BOOK IS
AVAILABLE FROM THE BRITISH LIBRARY.

ISBN: 978-0-75373-107-9

© BAUER MEDIA PTY LTD 2016

ABN 18 053 273 546

WINTER EXPRESS

Easy & delicious **COMFORT FOOD** ready in a flash

ℬℬ **Bounty**
Books

Contents

COMFORT *fast*

AS WINTER APPROACHES, WE FIND OURSELVES CRAVING RICH AND HEARTY FOOD TO COMBAT THE BITE OF THE COLD. BUT IN OUR FAST MOVING LIVES, IT SOMETIMES SEEMS IMPOSSIBLE TO FIND THE TIME TO GET INTO THE KITCHEN AND MAKE THESE COMFORTING DISHES. THIS BOOK SHOWS THAT EVEN IF YOU ARE TIME POOR, YOU CAN CREATE DELICIOUS MEALS THAT WILL SATISFY YOU AND YOUR FAMILY.

Quick comfort food

You don't have to stress to create flavoursome food this winter. This book is full of recipes for beautiful stews, soups, grills, roasts and desserts, all ready to be served in an hour or less. Each recipe is tested at least three times in The Australian Women's Weekly Test Kitchen to ensure you get the most out of your limited time. From spice-filled curries, quick vegie-packed pastas, family-friendly grills, and of course, recipes for warm, luscious desserts to finish up the night, there is something for everyone to love.

Smart shopping

With consumers becoming more health conscious and food savvy, there has never been a better time to find good-quality, ready-made products to speed up the cooking process. Embrace pre-made sauces, pastes and curries and opt for microwaveable grains, pre-made pizza bases and marinated and diced meats. Look for basic ingredients that can be used in different meals. For example, beef mince can become a taco filling, a hearty meat pie or a classic bolognese sauce. It is common to see peeled, chopped fresh vegetables, mixed salad leaves and roasted chickens in supermarkets. Make use of convenience products without skimping on health benefits. Ready-cooked rice is nutritionally equal to rice cooked from scratch, so too are ready-made sauces like pesto and hummus. Become familiar with brands that offer the most authentic tastes. Sometimes all you need to transform a meal from bland to brilliant is a simple marinade or dressing.

Meat & veg

Many traditional winter recipes use tougher cuts of meat cooked over a long period to make them tender and delicious. To speed it up, many of our recipes instead use leaner and more tender cuts, which will give equal flavour but will halve the cook and preparation time. Chicken and seafood also have a much quicker cooking time, and can be purchased pre-cooked ready to be added to your base sauce or stew. In the case of seafood, you can readily buy it prepared at most supermarkets. This book also contains many vegetarian recipes, which are both nutritious and budget friendly. Vegetables should make up the majority of any diet, and can easily bulk up a curry or pasta, or be the base for a hearty soup.

Essential tools

Useful modern kitchen utensils and appliances make it easier to multi-task, prepping ingredients and getting along with the cooking, to get dinner on your plate faster. Some of the Test Kitchen's favourite tools include a V-slicer or a mandoline, food processor, blender, sharp knives, scissors, a sharp vegetable peeler and a really sharp grater. Electrical appliances such as pressure cookers and microwaves are a great help in completing each step faster, either cooking potatoes, defrosting meat or in the case of the pressure cooker, making the perfect risotto, soup or stew.

Before you start

Ensure the kitchen is always stocked; dedicate one day a week to preparing a realistic weekly menu and shopping list. This way you are not pressed to think of what to cook after a busy and tiring day. Sunday is

groceries fortnightly or monthly to ensure the pantry is always stocked with commonly used ingredients such as rice, flour and pasta. Keep a chart of seasonal fruit and vegetables handy – this produce is usually available at a cheaper price as it's fresh and in plentiful supply. Make a note on your computer or smart phone of those items you frequently purchase, so you never forget everyday needs. Check the pantry first and compile a grocery list, grouping similar ingredients, so you only buy what you need.

Work like a pro

The easiest way to ensure that you cook fast and efficiently is to plan ahead, know your recipe and have your workspace organised – like a professional chef. Read your recipe from start to finish before even picking up a knife, to understand its flow and the ingredients you will need. It is often best to lay out your ingredients, in the order that you will need them, doing any trimming or slicing as necessary. Take out pots, pans and other equipment needed for the recipe. Fill the kettle and get it boiling, ready to pour into the pan. Preheat the oven or grill or heat

IN SEASON, READILY AVAILABLE FRESH INGREDIENTS ARE GREAT FOR BUDGET CONSCIOUS COOKS.

MEALS WITH KIDS IN MIND – NOT SO SPICY, NOT TOO MUCH CHILLI, BUT STILL FULL OF FLAVOUR.

THIS BUTTON TAKES ALL THE GUESS WORK OUT OF TRYING TO FIND FAST, HEALTHY FOOD CHOICES.

GREAT FOR THOSE NIGHTS YOU CAN'T BE BOTHERED WITH MULTIPLE POTS, PANS AND WASHING UP.

NOT JUST FOR MONDAYS – MEAT-FREE IS A GREAT WAY TO START EATING MORE FRESH VEGIES.

often a good day for full-time workers to plan next week's menu. Planning your shopping helps reduce waste as well, stopping impulse purchases and buying duplicate ingredients.

Bulk shop weekly

Save time by doing a regular bulk shop. Highly perishable items, such as fish, need to be purchased close to the time of cooking, however, it's great to buy large amounts of dry

Stock the pantry

A clean, organised pantry helps you find items quickly. Opened items should be at the front of the cupboard so they are at hand when needed. Mark the date on packets, so you know when it's time to discard them. Have a selection of staples, such as canned beans, tomatoes and tuna on hand. Keep a selection of condiments as these are the flavour builders of a meal – Asian sauces, spices, mustards, vinegars and oils are a must.

oil in the frying pan. Doing a little preparation like this can cut out much of the fussing, so you can concentrate on the food itself.

Getting the hang of it

Quick and efficient cooking only comes with practice. Some recipes will always require long cooking times, but as you become more confident in the kitchen, you can prove that it's easy to create warm and nourishing food in almost no time at all.

EXPRESS SOUPS & STEWS

Hot & sour
CHICKEN NOODLE SOUP

PREP & COOK TIME 25 MINUTES   SERVES 4

1½ cups (375ml) chicken stock

1.5 litres (6 cups) water

3 fresh kaffir lime leaves, torn in half

10cm (4-inch) stick fresh lemon grass (20g), halved lengthways

3cm (1¼-inch) piece fresh ginger (15g), sliced thinly

⅓ cup (75g) tom yum paste

2 tablespoons fish sauce

½ cup (125ml) lime juice

⅓ cup (75g) firmly packed brown sugar

200g (6½ ounces) dried rice stick noodles

400g (12½ ounces) baby buk choy, quartered

200g (6½ ounces) fresh shiitake mushrooms, sliced thinly

400g (12½ ounces) chicken breast fillets, sliced thinly

3 fresh small red thai (serrano) chillies, sliced thinly

¼ cup loosely packed fresh coriander (cilantro) leaves

1 Place stock, the water, lime leaves, lemon grass and ginger in a large saucepan; bring to the boil. Reduce heat; simmer, covered, for 5 minutes. Remove lemon grass and ginger with a slotted spoon. Stir in paste; return to the boil. Stir in the sauce, juice and sugar.
2 Meanwhile, place noodles in a large heatproof bowl; cover with boiling water, stand for 5 minutes or until tender. Drain.
3 Add buk choy to the stock mixture with mushrooms, chicken and two of the sliced chillies; simmer, uncovered, until chicken is cooked through. Stir in noodles; simmer, uncovered, until hot. Season to taste.
4 Serve soup topped with remaining chilli, coriander, and a squeeze of lime, if you like.

tips To save time, you can use chicken stir-fry strips instead of the breast fillet. Recipe is not suitable to freeze.

Quick & easy
BOUILLABAISSE

PREP & COOK TIME 15 MINUTES SERVES 4

2 cloves garlic

1 litre (4 cups) fish stock

2 x 8cm (3¼-inch) pieces orange rind

2 sprigs fresh thyme

pinch saffron threads

2 tablespoons olive oil

1 medium fennel bulb (300g), trimmed, sliced thinly, fronds reserved

1 small brown onion (80g), chopped coarsely

4 uncooked medium prawns (shrimp) (130g), unshelled

600g (1¼ pounds) marinara mix

1 long french bread stick (300g), cut into 1cm (½-inch) slices

250g (8 ounces) cherry truss tomatoes

20g (¾ ounce) butter

⅓ cup (100g) aïoli

¼ teaspoon cayenne pepper

1 Peel garlic. Keep one clove whole, crush other clove. Combine stock, rind, thyme, whole garlic and saffron in a medium saucepan; bring to the boil. Reduce heat; simmer, covered, about 4 minutes.

2 Meanwhile, heat oil in a large saucepan over medium-high heat; cook fennel, onion and crushed garlic, stirring, about 2 minutes or until softened. Add prawns and marinara mix; cook, stirring gently, until prawns are almost cooked.

3 Preheat a grill plate (or grill or barbecue) over high heat. Toast bread on grill plate until browned lightly.

4 Cook tomatoes on same heated oiled grill plate about 5 minutes or until just softened.

5 Meanwhile, strain stock mixture into marinara mixture; bring to the boil. Remove from heat, stir in butter. Season to taste. Divide bouillabaisse into serving bowls; top each bowl with grilled tomatoes and reserved fennel fronds. Sprinkle aïoli with cayenne. Serve bouillabaisse with toast and aïoli.

tip Use the best fish stock you can get for this recipe as the flavour relies on a good stock.

Spicy eggplant with
SOFT-BOILED EGGS & LABNE

PREP & COOK TIME 30 MINUTES SERVES 4

2 tablespoons extra virgin olive oil

1 large eggplant (500g), cut into 2.5cm (1-inch) pieces

1 large brown onion (200g), chopped coarsely

1 fresh long red chilli, sliced thinly

2 cloves garlic, crushed

2 teaspoons ground cumin

1 teaspoon ground coriander

400g (12½ ounces) canned chickpeas (garbanzo beans), drained, rinsed

800g (1½ pounds) canned diced tomatoes

1 cup (250ml) vegetable stock

8 eggs

1 loaf turkish bread (430g), halved

160g (5 ounces) drained labne

80g (2½ ounces) baby spinach leaves

½ teaspoon sumac

1 Heat half the oil in a large saucepan over high heat; cook eggplant, stirring, until browned and tender. Remove from pan.

2 Heat remaining oil in same pan; cook onion and chilli, stirring, until soft. Add garlic, cumin and coriander; cook, stirring, until fragrant.

3 Return eggplant to pan with chickpeas, tomatoes and stock; simmer, covered, for 15 minutes. Season to taste.

4 Meanwhile, place eggs in another large saucepan; cover with cold water. Cover pan with lid; bring to the boil. Boil eggs, uncovered, for 2 minutes. Drain immediately. Run eggs under cold water until cool enough to handle. Peel eggs.

5 Preheat a grill plate (or grill or barbecue) over high heat. Toast bread, cut-side down, on grill plate until browned lightly.

6 Divide eggplant mixture between shallow serving bowls; top with halved eggs, labne and spinach leaves. Sprinkle with sumac; serve with torn grilled bread.

tip To get a perfectly centred yolk in boiled eggs, gently stir the eggs with a wooden spoon until the water comes to the boil.

Chilli, lamb &
MANGO CURRY

PREP & COOK TIME 25 MINUTES   SERVES 4

100g (3 ounces) sugar snap peas, trimmed

1 tablespoon peanut oil

2 tablespoons yellow curry paste

400ml canned coconut cream

500g (1 pound) lamb backstrap (eye of loin),
cut into 1cm (½-inch) thick strips

1 large mango (600g), sliced thinly

1 large zucchini (150g), halved lengthways, sliced thinly

1 fresh long red chilli, sliced thinly diagonally

¼ cup vietnamese mint leaves

½ cup loosely packed fresh coriander (cilantro) leaves

1 cup (80g) bean sprouts, trimmed

1 lime, cut into wedges

1 Blanch peas in boiling water for 30 seconds; drain. Refresh under cold water. Cut in half lengthways.
2 Heat oil in a medium saucepan over medium-high heat. Add paste; cook, stirring for 1 minute or until fragrant. Stir in coconut cream; bring to the boil. Reduce heat; simmer, uncovered, for 3 minutes or until reduced slightly.
3 Add lamb to sauce; simmer, uncovered, for 4 minutes or until lamb is just cooked. Add peas, mango, zucchini and half the chilli; cook, stirring, until heated through.
4 Serve curry topped with mint, coriander and remaining chilli and with bean sprouts and lime wedges.

serving suggestions Serve with roti, or any flatbread you prefer, and mango pickle.
tip You can replace the lamb with pork fillet or chicken breast fillet, if you prefer; adjust the cooking time appropriately.

Mussels WITH CIDER

PREP & COOK TIME 15 MINUTES SERVES 2

340ml bottle cider

1 clove garlic, crushed

1kg (2 pounds) pot-ready mussels

1 cup (250ml) pouring cream

1 medium zucchini (120g), cut into long matchsticks

1 tablespoon fresh tarragon leaves

¼ cup finely chopped fresh chives

1 Bring cider to the boil in a large saucepan. Add garlic and mussels; cover, cook for 3 minutes, shaking pan occasionally, or until mussels open. Transfer mussels to a serving bowl.

2 Stir cream into pan; bring to the boil. Reduce heat to low; simmer, uncovered, for 5 minutes or until thickened slightly. Add zucchini and herbs; season. Spoon sauce over mussels.

serving suggestion Serve with a rocket (arugula) salad and crusty bread.

tip Use a mandoline or V-slicer with a julienne attachment to cut the zucchini into matchsticks.

One
PAN

Malaysian
FISH CURRY

PREP & COOK TIME 15 MINUTES SERVES 6

1 tablespoon vegetable oil

2 medium potatoes (400g), cut into wedges (see tip)

500g (1 pound) firm white fish fillets, cut into 2.5cm (1-inch) pieces

1 medium brown onion (150g), sliced thinly

1 clove garlic, crushed

1 cinnamon stick

2 x 410g (12½ ounces) canned mild malaysian curry sauce

200g (6½ ounces) green beans or sugar snap peas, trimmed, halved lengthways

750g (1½ pounds) packaged white long-grain microwave rice

⅓ cup (45g) roasted peanuts, chopped coarsely

½ cup coarsely chopped fresh coriander (cilantro)

1 Heat oil in a large deep frying pan over high heat; cook potatoes, in batches, until browned all over. Remove from pan. Add fish to pan, in batches; cook until browned. Remove from pan.

2 Cook onion and garlic in same pan, stirring, until onion softens. Return potatoes to pan with cinnamon and sauce; bring to the boil. Reduce heat; simmer, uncovered, about 5 minutes or until potato is tender. Add fish; simmer, uncovered, for 1 minute or until fish is cooked through.

3 Meanwhile, microwave beans until just tender.

4 Microwave rice according to directions on packet. Remove cinnamon stick from curry. Serve curry topped with beans, nuts and coriander; accompany with rice.

tip We used desiree potatoes for this recipe and left the skins on; use any potato you like. Baby new potatoes (chats), would also work well.

Chicken & corn CHOWDER

PREP & COOK TIME 40 MINUTES SERVES 4

2 cups (500ml) chicken stock

2 cups (500ml) water

2 chicken breast fillets (400g)

40g (1½ ounces) butter

1 large brown onion (200g), chopped finely

2 rindless bacon slices (130g), chopped coarsely

2 cloves garlic, crushed

2 tablespoons plain (all-purpose) flour

3 cups (750ml) milk, warmed

2 trimmed corn cobs (500g), kernels removed

2 medium potatoes (400g), chopped coarsely

2 tablespoons coarsely chopped chives

2 tablespoons micro cress or chervil

1 Bring stock and the water to the boil in a medium saucepan; add chicken, return to the boil. Reduce heat; simmer, covered, for 10 minutes or until chicken is cooked through. Cool chicken in poaching liquid for 5 minutes. Remove chicken from pan; shred coarsely. Reserve 2 cups (500ml) of the poaching liquid.

2 Melt butter in a large saucepan over medium heat, add onion, bacon and garlic; cook, stirring, for 5 minutes or until onion softens. Add flour; cook, stirring, until mixture thickens and bubbles. Gradually stir in warmed milk and reserved poaching liquid; stir until mixture boils and thickens slightly. Add corn and potato, reduce heat; simmer, covered, for 15 minutes or until potato is tender.

3 Add the shredded chicken; simmer, covered, until chicken is heated through. Season to taste. Serve chowder topped with chives and micro herbs.

serving suggestion Serve with crusty sourdough.
tip To save time, you can use 2½ cups (400g) shredded barbecued chicken; omit step 1, add 2 cups warmed chicken stock instead of the reserved poaching liquid with the milk in step 2 and add the shredded chicken as described in step 3.

Combination
SHORT SOUP

Healthy
CHOICE

Combination
SHORT SOUP

PREP & COOK TIME 40 MINUTES SERVES 4

1 litre (4 cups) water

500g (1 pound) chicken breast fillets

200g (6½ ounces) uncooked small prawns (shrimp)

2 litres (8 cups) chicken stock

1 tablespoon soy sauce

2 teaspoons finely grated fresh ginger

12 prawn and chive wontons (240g) (see tips)

200g (6½ ounces) chinese barbecued pork, sliced thinly

100g (3 ounces) mixed mushrooms, sliced thinly

2 baby pak choy (300g), trimmed, quartered

4 green onions (scallions), sliced thinly

1 fresh long red chilli, sliced thinly

1¼ cups (100g) bean sprouts

⅓ cup loosely packed fresh coriander (cilantro) leaves

1 lime, cut into wedges

1 Bring the water to the boil in a large saucepan; add chicken, return to the boil. Reduce heat; simmer, covered, for 10 minutes or until chicken is cooked. Cool chicken in poaching liquid for 10 minutes. Remove chicken from pan; discard poaching liquid. When cool enough to handle, slice chicken thinly.

2 Meanwhile, peel and devein prawns, leaving tails intact.

3 Bring stock, sauce and ginger to the boil in same cleaned pan. Add wontons; simmer, uncovered, for 5 minutes. Add chicken, prawns, pork and mushroom; reduce heat, simmer, uncovered, about 5 minutes or until prawns change colour and soup is hot. Stir in pak choy. Season to taste.

4 Serve soup topped with onion, chilli, sprouts and coriander. Serve with lime wedges.

tips Prepared wontons are available in the freezer section of large supermarkets and Asian food stores – you can use your favourite for this recipe. Chinese barbecued pork has a sweet, sticky coating. It is available from Asian grocery stores. Recipe is not suitable to freeze.

Kumara soup
WITH KALE CHIPS

PREP & COOK TIME 35 MINUTES **SERVES** 4

2 tablespoons extra virgin olive oil

1 medium brown onion (150g), chopped coarsely

2 cloves garlic, crushed

1 teaspoon ground cumin

pinch mexican chilli powder

600g (1¼ pounds) kumara (orange sweet potato), chopped coarsely

2 medium potatoes (400g), chopped coarsely

2 cups (500ml) water

1½ cups (375ml) vegetable stock

½ cup (125ml) pouring cream

1 tablespoon lemon juice

kale chips

200g (6½ ounces) green kale

1 tablespoon extra virgin olive oil

½ teaspoon crushed sea salt flakes

1 Heat half the oil in a large saucepan over medium-high heat; cook onion and garlic, stirring, about 5 minutes or until onion softens. Add spices; cook, stirring, for 1 minute or until fragrant. Add kumara, potato, the water and stock; bring to the boil. Reduce heat; simmer, covered, about 20 minutes or until vegetables are tender. Cool soup for 10 minutes.

2 Meanwhile, make kale chips.

3 Blend or process soup, in batches, until smooth. Return soup to same pan; add cream and juice. Reheat, stirring, without boiling, until hot. Season to taste.

4 Serve bowls of soup topped with kale chips; drizzle with remaining oil.

kale chips Preheat oven to 190°C/375°F. Place a large oven tray in the oven while preheating. Strip kale from stems. Wash kale well; pat dry with paper towel or in a salad spinner. Tear kale leaves into 5cm (2-inch) pieces; place in a large bowl, then drizzle with oil and sprinkle with salt. Rub salt and oil through the kale. Spread kale in a single layer on tray. Bake for 10 minutes. Remove pieces of kale that are crisp. Bake remaining kale for a further 2 minutes then remove crisp pieces. Repeat until all the kale is crisp. Cool.

tip You need about half a bunch of kale for this recipe.

Beef, barley &
CAVOLO NERO SOUP

PREP & COOK TIME 40 MINUTES SERVES 4

You will need a pressure cooker for this recipe.

1 tablespoon olive oil

1kg (2 pounds) beef chuck steak, cut into
2cm (¾ inch) pieces

½ cup (100g) pearl barley

1 large brown onion (200g), chopped coarsely

2 cloves garlic, crushed

2 stalks celery (300g), trimmed, chopped coarsely

1 large carrot (180g), sliced thickly

1 litre (4 cups) water

2 cups (500ml) beef stock

3 cups (240g) coarsely shredded cavolo nero
(tuscan cabbage)

¾ cup coarsely chopped fresh flat-leaf parsley

1 Heat oil in a 6-litre (24-cup) pressure cooker; cook beef, in batches, until browned. Remove from cooker.

2 Return beef to cooker with barley, onion, garlic, celery, carrot, the water and stock; secure lid. Bring cooker to high pressure. Reduce heat to stabilise pressure (see tips); cook for 25 minutes.

3 Release pressure using the quick release method (see tips); remove lid. Add cavolo nero to cooker; secure lid. Bring cooker to high pressure. Reduce heat to stabilise pressure (see tips); cook for 5 minutes.

4 Release pressure using the quick release method (see tips); remove lid. Stir in parsley; season to taste.

tips If you have an electric pressure cooker you won't need to reduce the heat to stabilise pressure, your cooker will automatically stabilise itself. Always check with the manufacturer's instructions before using. For the quick release method referred to above, use tongs (steam can burn your fingers) to turn the pressure valve and release the steam. This will release the pressure quickly, before you remove the lid to either check the food or add more ingredients. Recipe is suitable to freeze.

Cauliflower, capsicum & CHICKPEA CURRY

PREP & COOK TIME 40 MINUTES   SERVES 4

2 tablespoons olive oil

1 medium brown onion (150g), sliced thickly

1 large red capsicum (bell pepper) (350g), sliced thickly

1 clove garlic, crushed

2 teaspoons finely grated fresh ginger

2 fresh small red thai chillies, chopped finely

1 teaspoon ground cumin

½ teaspoon ground turmeric

¼ teaspoon ground cardamom

¼ teaspoon ground fennel

1 small cauliflower (1kg), trimmed, sliced thickly

400g (12½ ounces) canned diced tomatoes

400ml canned coconut cream

1 cup (250ml) vegetable stock

1 tablespoon tomato paste

175g (5½ ounces) chopped green kale

400g (12½ ounces) canned chickpeas (garbanzo beans), drained, rinsed

½ cup loosely packed fresh small mint leaves

1 Heat oil in a large saucepan over medium-high heat; cook onion, capsicum, garlic, ginger and chilli, stirring, about 5 minutes or until onion softens. Add spices and cauliflower; cook, stirring, for 2 minutes.

2 Add tomatoes, coconut cream, stock and paste; bring to the boil. Reduce heat; simmer, uncovered, for 20 minutes. Add kale and chickpeas; simmer, uncovered, about 10 minutes or until vegetables are tender. Season to taste.

3 Serve bowls of curry sprinkled with mint.

serving suggestion Serve with steamed jasmine rice.

Fish PROVENÇALE

PREP & COOK TIME 35 MINUTES SERVES 4

¼ cup (60ml) olive oil

6 green onions (scallions), trimmed, cut into thirds

1 clove garlic, sliced thinly

4 x 200g (6½-ounce) perch fillets

1 tablespoon finely chopped fresh rosemary

1 tablespoon fresh lemon thyme leaves

500g (1 pound) mixed tomatoes, chopped coarsely

⅓ cup (80ml) dry white wine

⅓ cup (80ml) fish stock

⅓ cup (55g) seeded mixed olives

2 pickled jalapeños, halved lengthways

1 Heat oil in a large, deep frying pan over medium-high heat; cook onion and garlic, stirring, for 3 minutes or until onion softens.

2 Increase heat to high. Season fish; add fish to pan with herbs. Cook fish for 2 minutes each side or until browned lightly.

3 Add tomato, wine, stock, olives and jalapeño to pan; cook, over medium heat for 5 minutes or until fish is cooked. Season to taste.

serving suggestions Serve with a warm crusty baguette and a raddichio and rocket salad.

tip We used perch fillets but you can use any firm white fish cutlets, steaks or fillets you like.

Peri peri coconut
PORK CURRY

PREP & COOK TIME 40 MINUTES SERVES 4

1 tablespoon olive oil

1kg (2 pounds) pork fillets, chopped coarsely

1 medium brown onion (150g), chopped coarsely

¼ cup (60ml) sweet sherry

200g (6½ ounces) coconut curry sauce

120g (4 ounces) peri peri sauce

165ml can coconut milk

1 cup (250ml) water

200g (6½ ounces) broccolini, trimmed, halved

⅓ cup (25g) shredded coconut

500g (1 pound) packaged basmati microwave rice

¼ cup loosely packed fresh micro mint

1 teaspoon black sesame seeds

1 lime, cut into wedges

1 Heat oil in a large heavy-based saucepan over high heat; cook pork, in batches, until browned all over.

2 Add onion and sherry to pan with pork; cook, stirring, about 3 minutes or until onion softens. Add sauces, coconut milk and the water; bring to the boil. Reduce heat; simmer, covered, for 15 minutes. Stir in broccolini; simmer, covered, for 10 minutes or until pork is tender and cooked through. Cut pork into thin slices. Return to pan.

3 Meanwhile, stir coconut in a medium frying pan, over low heat, for 3 minutes or until golden. Remove coconut from the pan immediately to prevent over-browning.

4 Microwave rice according to directions on packet. Place rice in a medium bowl with coconut; stir to combine.

5 Serve curry topped with mint and seeds, accompanied with coconut rice and lime wedges.

Pork, pear, parsnip
& SAGE STEW

PREP & COOK TIME 30 MINUTES SERVES 4

You will need a pressure cooker for this recipe.

1 tablespoon olive oil

800g (1½ pounds) rindless pork belly, chopped coarsely

40g (1½ ounces) butter

1 medium leek (350g), sliced thinly

2 cloves garlic, crushed

⅓ cup (80ml) verjuice

¾ cup (180ml) chicken stock

8 fresh sage leaves

2 medium parsnips (500g), quartered

2 medium firm pears (460g), quartered

¼ cup loosely packed fresh sage leaves, extra

1 Heat oil in a 6-litre (24-cup) pressure cooker; cook pork, in batches, until browned. Remove from cooker.

2 Melt half the butter in cooker; cook leek and garlic, stirring, about 5 minutes or until leek softens. Return pork to cooker with verjuice, stock and sage; secure lid. Bring cooker to high pressure. Reduce heat to stabilise pressure (see tips); cook for 10 minutes.

3 Release pressure using the quick release method (see tips); remove lid. Add parsnip; secure lid. Bring cooker to high pressure. Reduce heat to stabilise pressure (see tips); cook for 3 minutes. Release pressure using the quick release method (see tips); remove lid. Add pear; secure lid. Bring cooker to high pressure. Reduce heat to stabilise pressure (see tips); cook for 2 minutes.

4 Meanwhile, melt remaining butter in a small frying pan; cook extra sage leaves until bright green and crisp. Drain on paper towel.

5 Release pressure using the quick release method (see tips); remove lid. Season to taste. Serve stew sprinkled with crisp sage leaves.

serving suggestions Serve with steamed spinach or sugar snap peas and crusty bread to mop up the juices.

tips If you have an electric pressure cooker you won't need to reduce the heat to stabilise pressure, your cooker will automatically stabilise itself. Always check with the manufacturer's instructions before using. For the quick release method referred to above, use tongs (steam can burn your fingers) to turn the pressure valve and release the steam. This will release the pressure quickly, before you remove the lid to either check the food or add more ingredients. Make sure you use firm pears for this recipe or they will become mushy. Stew is suitable to freeze.

Seafood chu
CHEE CURRY

¼ cup (60g) ghee

2½ tablespoons thai red curry paste

800g (1½ pounds) marinara mix

6 fresh kaffir lime leaves

270ml canned coconut milk

1 cup (250ml) fish stock

2 tablespoons coconut sugar

2 tablespoons fish sauce

1 tablespoon tamarind puree

225g (7 ounces) canned bamboo shoots, drained, rinsed

½ cup (85g) chopped fresh pineapple

250g (8-ounce) packet microwave white rice

1 fresh long red chilli, seeded, sliced finely

4 roti bread (500g), warmed

1 Heat a wok over medium-high heat. Add ghee and curry paste; cook, stirring, for 2 minutes or until fragrant. Add marinara mix and 3 crushed lime leaves; cook, stirring, for 2 minutes. Add coconut milk and stock, sugar, sauce and tamarind. Stir in bamboo shoots and pineapple; cook a further 5 minutes or until warmed though.

2 Meanwhile, heat rice following packet instructions.

3 Finely shred remaining lime leaves; combine with chilli. Sprinkle lime leaf mixture on curry; serve with rice and warm roti bread.

Spanish chicken
& CHORIZO STEW

PREP & COOK TIME 40 MINUTES SERVES 6

1 cup (250ml) chicken stock

pinch saffron threads

340g (11 ounces) cured chorizo sausage, sliced thickly

1.5kg (3 pounds) chicken drumsticks

2 teaspoons olive oil

1 medium brown onion (150g), sliced thickly

1 medium red capsicum (bell pepper) (200g), sliced thickly

2 teaspoons smoked paprika

800g (1½ pounds) canned crushed tomatoes

½ cup (75g) seeded black olives

¼ cup loosely packed fresh flat-leaf parsley leaves

1 Combine stock and saffron in a small bowl. Set aside until required.

2 Cook chorizo in a large saucepan, over medium heat, until browned. Drain on paper towel.

3 Cook chicken, in batches, in the same pan, for 3 minutes each side, or until browned all over. Remove from pan.

4 Heat oil in the same pan; cook onion and capsicum, stirring, about 2 minutes or until onion softens. Add paprika; cook, stirring, until fragrant.

5 Return chorizo and chicken to pan. Add stock mixture and tomatoes, cover; bring to the boil. Reduce heat; simmer, covered, about 20 minutes or until chicken is cooked through. Stir in olives.

6 Serve stew sprinkled with parsley; accompany with crusty bread rolls, if you like.

Spicy beef in tomato
& SPINACH SAUCE

PREP & COOK TIME 40 MINUTES SERVES 4

You will need a pressure cooker for this recipe.

1 tablespoon vegetable oil

1kg (2 pounds) gravy beef, chopped coarsely

1 medium brown onion (150g), chopped finely

3 cloves garlic, crushed

2 fresh small red thai chillies, chopped finely

2 teaspoons ground coriander

2 teaspoons garam masala

1 teaspoon ground cumin

1 teaspoon ground fenugreek

½ teaspoon ground turmeric

410g (13 ounces) canned cherry tomatoes

½ cup (125ml) beef stock

100g (3 ounces) baby spinach leaves

⅓ cup loosely packed fresh coriander (cilantro) leaves

1 Heat half the oil in a 6-litre (24-cup) pressure cooker; cook beef, in batches, until browned. Remove from cooker.
2 Heat remaining oil in cooker; cook onion, garlic and chilli, stirring, until onion softens. Add spices; cook, stirring, until fragrant. Return beef to cooker with tomatoes and stock; secure lid. Bring cooker to high pressure. Reduce heat to stabilise pressure (see tips); cook for 25 minutes.
3 Release pressure using the quick release method (see tips); remove lid. Stir in spinach; season to taste. Serve sprinkled with coriander.

serving suggestion Serve with steamed basmati rice and warm naan.

tips If you have an electric pressure cooker you won't need to reduce the heat to stabilise pressure, your cooker will automatically stabilise itself. Always check with the manufacturer's instructions before using. For the quick release method referred to above, use tongs (steam can burn your fingers) to turn the pressure valve and release the steam. This will release the pressure quickly, before you remove the lid to either check the food or add more ingredients. Recipe suitable to freeze.

Green curry &
KAFFIR LIME PRAWN SOUP

PREP & COOK TIME 45 MINUTES   SERVES 4

1kg (2 pounds) uncooked medium prawns (shrimp)

1 tablespoon peanut oil

¼ cup (75g) green curry paste

1 litre (4 cups) chicken stock

800ml canned coconut milk

1 fresh long green chilli, chopped finely

8 fresh kaffir lime leaves

125g (4 ounces) rice vermicelli

125g (4 ounces) sugar snap peas, trimmed, halved lengthways

2 tablespoons grated palm sugar

2 tablespoons lime juice

2 tablespoons fish sauce

1 cup (80g) bean sprouts

½ cup loosely packed vietnamese mint leaves

1 fresh long green chilli, extra, sliced thinly

2 limes, cut into thin wedges

1 Shell and devein prawns, leaving tails intact. Heat oil in a large saucepan over medium heat; cook prawns, in batches, for 2 minutes or until browned lightly. Remove from pan.
2 Add paste to same pan; cook, stirring, about 2 minutes or until fragrant. Add stock, coconut milk, chopped chilli and 4 crushed lime leaves; bring to the boil. Reduce heat; simmer, uncovered, for 20 minutes. Return prawns to pan with vermicelli and peas; cook, uncovered, until vermicelli is just tender. Stir in sugar, juice and sauce. Season to taste.
3 Finely shred the remaining lime leaves. Serve soup sprinkled with shredded lime leaves, sprouts, mint and sliced chilli. Serve with lime wedges.

tips Vietnamese mint is not a mint, but a narrow-leafed, pungent herb, also known as laksa leaf. Recipe is not suitable to freeze.

Cheat's minestrone
WITH MEATBALLS

PREP & COOK TIME 1 HOUR   SERVES 6

6 italian-style pork and fennel sausages (675g)

2 tablespoons olive oil

1 medium brown onion (150g), chopped coarsely

1 clove garlic, crushed

¼ cup (70g) tomato paste

1.5 litres (6 cups) water

2 cups (500ml) chicken stock

2⅔ cups (700g) bottled passata

1 celery stalk (150g), trimmed, chopped coarsely

1 medium carrot (120g), chopped coarsely

1 medium zucchini (120g), chopped coarsely

80g (2½ ounces) green beans, trimmed, sliced diagonally

400g (12½ ounces) canned borlotti beans, drained, rinsed

¾ cup (135g) macaroni

⅓ cup loosely packed fresh small basil leaves

⅓ cup (25g) flaked parmesan

1 Squeeze sausage meat from casings into a medium bowl, discard casings. Roll sausage meat into 2cm (¾-inch) meatballs, using wet hands. Heat half the oil in a large saucepan over medium-high heat; cook meatballs, turning, about 5 minutes or until browned all over. Remove from pan.

2 Heat remaining oil in same pan; cook onion and garlic, stirring, about 5 minutes or until onion softens. Add paste; cook, stirring, 2 minutes. Add the water, stock and passata; bring to the boil.

3 Add celery to pan; simmer, uncovered, 10 minutes. Add carrot, zucchini and green beans; simmer, uncovered, about 20 minutes or until carrot is tender. Return meatballs to pan with borlotti beans and pasta; simmer, uncovered, stirring occasionally, about 10 minutes or until pasta is tender. Season to taste.

4 Serve soup topped with basil and parmesan.

tips This is a speedier version of this Italian classic, which usually uses dried beans and ham hocks and requires long cooking times. You could use a can of red kidney beans if you can't find canned borlotti beans.

Fennel & swede soup
WITH PEAR CRISPS

PREP & COOK TIME 1 HOUR SERVES 6

5 medium fennel bulbs (1.5kg)

2 tablespoons olive oil, plus extra to drizzle

1 medium leek (350g), chopped coarsely

2 celery stalks (300g), trimmed, chopped coarsely

1 medium swede (230g), grated coarsely

2 cloves garlic, crushed

1 large potato (300g)

3 cups (750ml) vegetable stock

2½ cups (625ml) water

1 cup (250ml) pouring cream

cinnamon pear crisps

1 small pear (180g)

2 tablespoons olive oil

1 teaspoon caster (superfine) sugar

pinch ground cinnamon

1 Trim fennel, reserving fronds. Coarsely chop fennel.

2 Heat oil in a large saucepan over medium heat; cook fennel, stirring, until soft. Add leek, celery and swede; cook, stirring occasionally, about 15 minutes or until vegetables begin to caramelise. Stir in garlic; cook, stirring, for 1 minute or until fragrant.

3 Coarsely grate peeled potato, add to pan with stock and the water; bring to the boil. Reduce heat; simmer, covered, about 20 minutes or until vegetables are tender. Cool 10 minutes.

4 Meanwhile, make cinnamon pear crisps.

5 Reserve some of the braised celery pieces. Blend or process soup, in batches, until smooth. Season to taste. Strain soup into pan, add half the cream; heat soup over medium heat, stirring occasionally, until hot.

6 Ladle soup into serving bowls; top with reserved celery and pear crisps. Drizzle with remaining cream and extra oil, and sprinkle with reserved fennel fronds.

cinnamon pear crisps Using a mandoline or V-slicer, finely slice pear lengthways. Heat oil in a large frying pan over medium-high heat; cook pear, in batches, about 30 seconds each side or until golden and crisp. Drain on paper towel. While still warm sprinkle with combined sugar and cinnamon.

tips Before using, wash leeks under running water to remove any grit from the inside layers. A firm pear, such as corella, is best for this recipe. The pear slices will become crisper when cool. Recipe is not suitable to freeze.

Speedy
LAMB CURRY
PREP & COOK TIME 50 MINUTES
SERVES 4

Cook 1 finely chopped large onion (200g) in a heated oiled large saucepan over medium-high heat, stirring, about 5 minutes or until soft and browned lightly. Add ⅓ cup (100g) balti curry paste and 1kg (2lb) diced lamb; cook, stirring, until lamb is browned all over. Add 410g (12½oz) canned diced tomatoes and ⅓ cup (80ml) water; bring to the boil. Simmer, covered, about 30 minutes or until lamb is tender. Add 125g (4oz) baby spinach leaves; simmer until spinach wilts. Season to taste. Serve topped with fresh small mint leaves, accompanied with steamed basmati rice.

tip Balti curry paste is a medium-hot paste containing coriander, fenugreek and mint, which gives it a distinctive mild "green" flavour.

Mexican chorizo
& BEAN STEW
PREP & COOK TIME 30 MINUTES
SERVES 4

Cook 6 fresh chorizo sausages (675g) in a heated oiled large frying pan. Remove from pan. Drain and rinse 800g (1½lb) canned four-bean mix. Add drained beans, 30g (1oz) packet taco seasoning, 410g (12½oz) canned diced tomatoes, ½ cup (120g) thickly sliced roasted red capsicum (bell pepper), 1 cup (160g) fresh or frozen corn kernels and ⅓ cup (80ml) water to the same pan; bring to the boil. Reduce heat; simmer, uncovered, about 5 minutes or until sauce thickens. Meanwhile, slice sausages thickly; return to pan, simmer, uncovered, until heated through. Season to taste. Serve sprinkled with ¼ cup firmly packed fresh small coriander (cilantro) leaves. Accompany with grilled tortillas and sour cream, if you like.

FAST STEWS

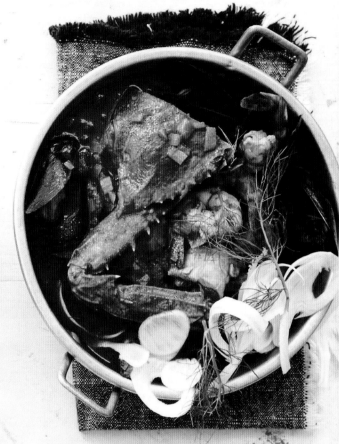

Creamy tomato
CHICKEN CACCIATORE
PREP & COOK TIME 20 MINUTES
SERVES 4

Heat 1 tablespoon olive oil in a medium saucepan over high heat; cook 500g (1lb) thinly sliced chicken breast, in batches, until browned. Remove from pan. Heat another 1 tablespoon olive oil in same pan; cook 150g (5oz) thinly sliced portobello mushrooms and 1 crushed garlic clove, stirring occasionally, about 5 minutes or until mushrooms are tender. Return chicken to pan with 400g (12½oz) canned crushed tomatoes. Simmer, uncovered, for 5 minutes or until chicken is cooked through. Add ½ cup (125ml) pouring cream, ⅓ cup (60g) coarsely chopped seeded black olives; simmer, uncovered, for 1 minute. Season to taste. Serve with cooked farfalle (bowtie) pasta or creamy polenta. Sprinkle with fresh oregano leaves.

Lemon & fennel
SEAFOOD STEW
PREP & COOK TIME 45 MINUTES
SERVES 6

Trim 2 baby fennel bulbs (260g); reserve fronds. Using a V-slicer or mandoline, finely slice fennel; combine with 2 tablespoons lemon juice in a small bowl. Cook 1 finely chopped large brown onion (200g) in a heated oiled large saucepan, stirring, about 5 minutes or until soft. Add 4 crushed garlic cloves; cook, stirring, for 1 minute. Add ⅓ cup (80ml) dry white wine, pinch each of dried chilli flakes and saffron threads; cook, stirring, for 2 minutes. Add 800g (1½lb) canned diced tomatoes; simmer, uncovered, for about 10 minutes or until mixture thickens slightly. Add 1 litre (4 cups) fish stock; simmer, uncovered, for about 20 minutes or until liquid is reduced by about a quarter. Add 2kg (4lb) marinara mix. Cover; simmer, stirring occasionally, about 5 minutes or until prawns change colour. Serve stew topped with fennel mixture; sprinkle with reserved fronds, accompany with crusty bread.

EXPRESS BAKES & ROASTS

One-pan
SAUSAGE BAKE

PREP & COOK TIME 40 MINUTES   SERVES 4

8 thick beef sausages (1.2kg)

2 medium yellow capsicums (bell peppers) (400g), sliced thickly

1 small red onion (100g), cut into wedges

375g (12 ounces) cherry tomatoes

2 cups (500ml) water

1 cup (170g) instant polenta (cornmeal)

¾ cup (180ml) pouring cream

¼ cup (20g) finely grated parmesan

¼ cup loosely packed fresh small basil leaves

1 Preheat oven to 200°C/400°F.

2 Heat a large flameproof baking dish over high heat. Cook sausages until browned all over. Add capsicum and onion; season.

3 Roast, uncovered, for 15 minutes. Add tomatoes, roast for a further 15 minutes or until sausages are cooked through and the vegetables are tender.

4 Meanwhile, bring the water to the boil in a medium saucepan. Stir in polenta, reduce heat to low; cook, stirring, for 10 minutes or until polenta thickens. Stir in cream; cook, stirring, for 5 minutes or until polenta thickens. Stir in parmesan; season to taste.

5 Serve sausages and vegetables with polenta. Sprinkle with basil.

serving suggestion Serve with a mixed leaf salad.

Kid
FRIENDLY

Baked prawns
WITH FETTA

PREP & COOK TIME 45 MINUTES SERVES 4

1kg (2 pounds) uncooked medium king prawns (shrimp)

1 tablespoon olive oil

1 medium brown onion (150g), sliced thinly

2 cloves garlic, crushed

400g (13 ounces) bottled passata

few drops Tabasco

100g (3 ounces) fetta, crumbled

2 tablespoons coarsely chopped fresh flat-leaf parsley

fresh crusty bread, to serve

1 Preheat oven to 180°C/350°F.

2 Shell and devein prawns, leaving tails intact.

3 Combine prawns, oil, onion, garlic, passata and Tabasco in a 1 litre (4-cup) ovenproof dish; season. Sprinkle with fetta. Bake uncovered, about 30 minutes or until prawns are cooked through.

4 Sprinkle prawns with parsley; serve with bread.

serving suggestion Serve with a leafy green salad.

Creamy chicken
& CORN BURRITOS

PREP & COOK TIME 35 MINUTES SERVES 4

1¼ cups loosely packed fresh coriander (cilantro) leaves

310g (10 ounces) canned corn kernels, drained, rinsed

3 cups (480g) shredded cooked chicken (see tips)

2 cups (240g) coarsely grated cheddar

1 cup (240g) light sour cream

1 clove garlic, crushed

½ teaspoon cayenne pepper

8 x 20cm (8-inch) flour tortillas

2 limes, cut in half or wedges

1 Preheat oven to 220°C/425°F. Oil a large ovenproof dish.

2 Coarsely chop ¼ cup of the coriander. Combine corn, chopped coriander, chicken, 1 cup of the cheddar, sour cream, garlic and half the cayenne in a medium bowl; season to taste.

3 To make burritos, divide chicken mixture evenly among tortillas; roll to enclose filling, folding in sides. Place burritos in dish; sprinkle with remaining cheddar and remaining cayenne pepper. Bake, uncovered, about 25 minutes or until browned lightly.

4 Sprinkle burritos with remaining coriander; serve with lime wedges.

serving suggestion Serve with a tomato and avocado salad.
tips You can use 1 cup thawed frozen corn kernels instead of canned, if you prefer. It is fine to use shredded barbecued chicken in this recipe. A large (900g/1¾-pound) chicken should give 3 cups of shredded chicken meat.

Honey-mustard beef WITH MACADAMIA RICE

PREP & COOK TIME 40 MINUTES SERVES 4

600g (1¼-pound) piece scotch fillet

⅓ cup (95g) honeycup mustard

400g (12½ ounces) baby heirloom carrots, trimmed

400g (12½ ounces) spring onions, trimmed to 10cm (4-inch) lengths

1 tablespoon olive oil

¼ cup (60ml) thickened (heavy) cream

macadamia rice

20g (¾ ounce) butter

1 medium brown onion (150g), sliced thinly

1 clove garlic, crushed

2 teaspoons yellow mustard seeds

1 cup (200g) basmati rice

1 cup (125ml) chicken stock

1 cup (125ml) water

1 cup coarsely chopped fresh flat-leaf parsley

½ cup (70g) coarsely chopped roasted macadamias

1 Preheat oven to 240°C/475°F.

2 Place beef in a large baking dish; brush all over with half the mustard. Add carrots and onions to dish; drizzle with oil, season. Roast about 35 minutes or until beef is cooked as desired and vegetables are tender. Remove from oven; cover to keep warm.

3 Meanwhile, make macadamia rice.

4 Heat remaining mustard and cream in a small saucepan. Season to taste.

5 Serve sliced beef, drizzled with sauce, with vegetables and macadamia rice.

macadamia rice Melt butter in a medium saucepan over medium-high heat; cook onion, garlic and seeds, stirring, about 5 minutes or until onion softens. Add rice; cook, stirring, for 1 minute. Stir in stock and the water; bring to the boil. Reduce heat; simmer, covered, about 25 minutes or until rice is just tender. Remove from heat; fluff rice with a fork, stir in parsley and nuts. Season to taste.

Cajun roast chicken
WITH CORN CREAM

PREP & COOK TIME 35 MINUTES   SERVES 4

4 chicken breast supremes (1kg)

2 tablespoons olive oil

2 tablespoons cajun seasoning

1 clove garlic

500g (1 pound) frozen corn kernels

1 cup (240g) sour cream

1 cup (250ml) pouring cream

175g (5½ ounces) asparagus, halved lengthways

150g (4½ ounces) green beans, trimmed, halved lengthways

1 lime, cut into wedges

1 cup loosely packed fresh coriander (cilantro) leaves

1 Preheat oven to 200°C/400°F. Line an oven tray with baking paper.

2 Heat a large frying pan over medium-high heat. Combine chicken, oil and seasoning in a large bowl; season. Cook chicken, skin-side down, for 5 minutes or until browned. Transfer chicken, skin-side up to tray. Roast about 15 minutes or until chicken is cooked.

3 Meanwhile, place whole peeled garlic, corn, sour cream and cream in a medium saucepan; cook, stirring, until mixture boils. Reduce heat; simmer, uncovered, about 5 minutes or until mixture thickens. Remove from heat; blend with a stick blender until almost smooth. Season to taste.

4 Boil, steam or microwave asparagus and beans until tender; drain.

5 Serve chicken with creamed corn mixture, vegetables and lime. Sprinkle with coriander.

Kid FRIENDLY

Buttermilk chicken
MAC & CHEESE

PREP & COOK TIME 40 MINUTES SERVES 6

250g (8 ounces) macaroni pasta

1¼ cups (300g) sour cream

1½ cups (375ml) buttermilk

½ teaspoon ground nutmeg

2 cups (320g) shredded cooked chicken

1 cup (120g) frozen peas

1 teaspoon finely grated lemon rind

60g (2 ounces) baby spinach leaves

2½ cups (250g) pizza cheese

½ cup (35g) panko (japanese) breadcrumbs

1 tablespoon fresh thyme leaves

1 Preheat oven to 220°C/425°F. Oil a 2.5-litre (10-cup) ovenproof dish.

2 Cook pasta in a large saucepan of boiling water until tender; drain.

3 Heat sour cream and buttermilk in a large saucepan over low heat; stir in nutmeg, chicken, peas, rind, spinach and about three-quarters of the cheese, stir until smooth. Season.

4 Meanwhile, combine remaining cheese, breadcrumbs and thyme in a small bowl. Stir pasta into hot cheese sauce; spoon into dish. Sprinkle with breadcrumb mixture.

5 Bake about 20 minutes or until browned lightly.

serving suggestion Serve with a green leafy salad.

Quick roast pork with PEAR & APRICOT RELISH

410g (13 ounces) canned sliced pears in natural juice

410g (13 ounces) canned apricot halves in natural juice

½ cup (125ml) water

2 tablespoons white wine vinegar

1 fresh long red chilli, chopped finely

¼ cup (40g) sultanas

2 tablespoons white (granulated) sugar

600g (1¼ pounds) pork fillets

1 tablespoon olive oil

800g (1½ pounds) kumara (orange sweet potato), chopped coarsely

175g (5½ ounces) broccolini, trimmed

60g (1 ounce) butter

micro herbs, to serve

1 Drain pears over a small bowl. Reserve juice; chop pears coarsely. Drain apricots, discarding juice. Chop apricots coarsely. Combine pear, apricot, reserved juice, water, vinegar, chilli, saltanas and sugar in a medium saucepan; bring to the boil. Reduce heat; simmer, uncovered, stirring occasionally, for 20 minutes or until relish thickens slightly.

2 Brush pork with oil. Cook pork, on an heated oiled grill plate (or grill or barbecue) over medium-high heat for 3 minutes each side or until just cooked through. Remove from heat; stand, covered, for 5 minutes to rest then slice thickly.

3 Boil, steam or microwave kumara and broccolini, separately, until tender; drain. Mash kumara with butter until smooth. Season to taste.

4 Serve pork with relish, kumara mash and broccolini, topped with micro herbs.

Healthy CHOICE

Mustard & horseradish ROAST BEEF

PREP & COOK TIME 35 MINUTES   SERVES 4

650g (1¼ pounds) beef eye fillet

2 tablespoons olive oil

2 teaspoons wholegrain mustard

4 small beetroot (beets) (400g)

2 small kumara (orange sweet potato) (500g), cut into wedges

400g (12½ ounces) baby carrots, trimmed

1 medium red onion (170g), cut into wedges

170g (5½ ounces) asparagus, trimmed

60g (2 ounces) baby beetroot leaves

mustard horseradish dressing

2 teaspoons horseradish cream

1 small clove garlic, crushed

2 teaspoons wholegrain mustard

2 teaspoons red wine vinegar

¼ cup (60ml) olive oil

2 tablespoons light thickened (heavy) cream

1 Preheat oven to 240°C/475°F.

2 Rub beef all over with half the oil. Cook beef in a heated flameproof baking dish over high heat on the stove top until browned all over. Spread mustard all over beef; season. Transfer to oven; roast, uncovered, about 15 minutes or until beef is cooked as desired. Remove beef from dish; cover to keep warm.

3 Meanwhile, trim beetroot; cut in half (or quarters if large), then wrap in foil forming a parcel. Add beetroot to baking dish with beef for the last 10 minutes of beef cooking time.

4 Place kumara, carrots and onion on a baking-paper-lined large oven tray; transfer beetroot, still in foil, to tray with vegetables. Brush vegetables with remaining oil; season. Roast vegetables about 15 minutes or until tender and beginning to brown. Remove vegetables from tray as they are cooked.

5 Add asparagus to oven tray for last 5 minutes of cooking time or until just tender.

6 Make mustard horseradish dressing. Peel beetroot.

7 Place warm roast vegetables and beetroot leaves on a serving platter, drizzle with a little dressing. Slice beef thickly, arrange on top of vegetables; drizzle with dressing.

mustard horseradish dressing Whisk horseradish cream, garlic, mustard and vinegar in a medium bowl until combined. Gradually whisk in oil then cream. Season to taste.

serving suggestion Serve with roasted cherry truss tomatoes.
tips Dressing can be made a day ahead. The vegetables should be spread out in a single layer so they cook quickly.

Herb-crumbed BAKED BEANS

PREP & COOK TIME 35 MINUTES SERVES 4

1 medium brown onion (150g), chopped coarsely

100g (3 ounces) pancetta, chopped coarsely

¼ cup (60ml) olive oil

2 slices sourdough bread (140g), torn

½ cup (40g) finely grated parmesan

¼ cup loosely packed fresh oregano leaves

2 cloves garlic, crushed

1.2kg (2.5lb) canned white beans, drained, rinsed

1½ cups (375ml) bottled passata

1 tablespoon worcestershire sauce

¼ cup (60ml) pure maple syrup

2 teaspoons smoked paprika

1 Preheat oven to 220°C/425°F.

2 Combine onion, pancetta and 1 tablespoon of the oil in a 2-litre (8-cup) ovenproof dish. Bake, uncovered, about 15 minutes or until onion is browned lightly.

3 Meanwhile, combine bread, parmesan, oregano and remaining oil in a medium bowl.

4 Stir garlic, beans, sauces, maple syrup and paprika into pancetta mixture; season. Top with bread mixture. Bake, uncovered, about 10 minutes or until bread is browned.

serving suggestion Serve with baby rainbow radishes.

Plum-glazed duck
WITH ROASTED VEGETABLES

PREP & COOK TIME 35 MINUTES SERVES 4

400g (12½ ounces) baby heirloom carrots, trimmed

1 large red onion (300g), cut into wedges

170g (5½ ounces) asparagus, trimmed

2 teaspoons olive oil

4 x 150g (4½-ounce) duck breast fillets, skin on

¼ cup (90g) plum sauce

1 tablespoon sweet chilli sauce

200g (6½ ounces) baby vine-ripened truss tomatoes

1 Preheat oven to 180°C/350°F.

2 Combine carrots, onion, asparagus and oil on a large baking tray; season. Roast about 15 minutes or until vegetables are tender.

3 Meanwhile, place duck, skin-side down, in a large frying pan; cook, over medium heat, turning occasionally, until browned. Transfer to a large baking tray lined with baking paper.

4 Combine sauces in a small jug. Brush both sides of duck with sauce mixture; add tomatoes to baking tray. Roast duck and tomatoes for about 5 minutes or until tomatoes soften.

5 Serve duck and tomatoes with roasted vegetables.

tips Place the duck breast skin-side down in a cold frying pan, then turn on the heat; this helps render off some of the fat. You can use orange baby carrots if heirloom are unavailable.

Sun-dried tomato MEATLOAF

PREP & COOK TIME 50 MINUTES SERVES 4

750g (1½ pounds) minced (ground) veal

½ cup (130g) sun-dried tomato pesto

1 cup (70g) stale breadcrumbs

1 egg, beaten lightly

800g (1½ pounds) baby new potatoes

2 tablespoons olive oil

2 teaspoons fresh thyme leaves

300g (12½ ounces) spinach, trimmed

¼ cup (65g) sun-dried tomato pesto, extra

1 Preheat oven to 200°C/400°F. Line base and sides of an 11cm x 19cm (4½-inch x 7½-inch) loaf pan with baking paper.

2 Combine veal, pesto, breadcrumbs and egg in a large bowl; season. Press mixture into pan. Bake about 40 minutes or until cooked through. Stand 10 minutes before slicing.

3 Meanwhile, prick potatoes with a fork; place in a microwave-safe bowl. Microwave on HIGH (100%) for 3 minutes or until almost tender. Slice potatoes thinly.

4 Heat oil in a large frying pan over high heat; cook potato with thyme, in two batches, for 2 minutes each side or until golden. Remove from pan, season to taste; cover to keep warm.

5 Add spinach to pan, in two batches; cook, stirring, for 1 minute or until wilted. Season to taste.

6 Serve meatloaf with potatoes, spinach and extra pesto.

Lamb & mushroom
PIES WITH MUSHY PEAS

Kid
FRIENDLY

Lamb & mushroom
PIES WITH MUSHY PEAS

PREP & COOK TIME 40 MINUTES   SERVES 4

2 sheets shortcrust pastry

2 tablespoons olive oil

300g (9½ ounces) coarsely chopped mushrooms

500g (1 pound) minced (ground) lamb

1 cup (250g) bottled tomato and basil pasta sauce

1 egg, beaten lightly

500g (1 pound) frozen peas

30g (1 ounce) butter

1 tablespoon coarsely chopped fresh mint

1 Preheat oven to 180°C/350°F.

2 Cut one pastry sheet into four squares. Line four oiled 9.5cm (3½-inch) (base measurement) pie tins with pastry; trim excess pastry.

3 Heat oil in a large frying pan over medium-high heat; cook mushrooms, stirring occasionally, about 5 minutes or until golden. Add lamb; cook, stirring to break up lumps, for 5 minutes or until browned. Stir in sauce; season to taste.

4 Fill pastry cases with lamb mixture. Brush pastry edges with egg. Cut four rounds large enough to cover pie tops, from remaining pastry sheet; cover filling with pastry rounds, pressing edges together with a fork to seal. Brush pastry with egg. Make small cuts in tops of each pie; bake pies about 25 minutes or until browned.

5 Carefully, take pies out of tins; return pies to tray, cover loosely with foil. Bake pies, on bottom shelf of the oven, for 5 minutes or until pastry bases are cooked through.

6 Meanwhile, boil, steam or microwave peas until tender; drain. Blend or process peas with butter, mint and 1 tablespoon boiling water, pulsing, until crushed coarsely. Season to taste.

7 Serve pies with peas.

serving suggestion Serve with tomato sauce.

Snapper, potato wedges & HORSERADISH MAYO

PREP & COOK TIME 50 MINUTES **SERVES** 2

400g (12½ ounces) potatoes

6 cloves garlic

2 tablespoons olive oil

2 whole baby snapper (600g), cleaned

1 medium lemon (140g), sliced thinly

⅓ cup loosely packed fresh dill sprigs

2 teaspoons rinsed, drained capers

¼ cup (75g) mayonnaise

2 teaspoons horseradish cream

1 medium lemon (140g), extra, cut into cheeks

1 Preheat oven to 240°C/475°F.

2 Wash unpeeled potatoes; cut into wedges. Combine potato, unpeeled garlic and 1 tablespoon of the oil in a large baking dish; season. Roast, uncovered, for 20 minutes.

3 Meanwhile, fill fish cavities with lemon and ¼ cup of the dill; season. Place fish on top of potato; drizzle with remaining oil. Roast, uncovered, about 25 minutes or until fish and potato are cooked through.

4 Meanwhile, finely chop remaining dill and capers. Combine dill and capers with mayonnaise and horseradish cream in a small bowl.

5 Serve fish with potato, horseradish mayonnaise and extra lemon wedges.

serving suggestion Serve with a shaved fennel and mixed herb salad.

Salmon mornay pie
WITH CELERIAC MASH

PREP & COOK TIME 50 MINUTES SERVES 4

50g (1½ ounces) butter

1 medium brown onion (150g), sliced thinly

2 cloves garlic, crushed

¼ cup (35g) plain (all-purpose) flour

2 cups (500ml) milk, warmed

150g (4½ ounces) baby spinach leaves

415g (13 ounces) canned pink salmon, drained, flaked

2 tablespoons coarsely chopped fresh dill

2 teaspoons finely grated lemon rind

2 tablespoons lemon juice

¼ cup (20g) finely grated parmesan

dill sprigs, extra, to serve

potato and celeriac mash

400g (12½ ounces) potatoes, chopped coarsely

300g (12½ ounces) celeriac (celery root), chopped coarsely

2 tablespoons milk

30g (1 ounce) butter

⅓ cup (25g) finely grated parmesan

1 Preheat oven to 200°C/400°F. Grease a shallow 2-litre (8-cup) ovenproof dish.

2 Make potato and celeriac mash.

3 Meanwhile, melt butter in a medium saucepan over medium-high heat; cook onion and garlic, stirring, about 5 minutes or until onion softens. Add flour; cook, stirring, until mixture bubbles and thickens. Gradually stir in milk; cook, stirring, until mixture boils and thickens. Remove from heat; stir in spinach, salmon, dill, rind and juice. Season to taste.

4 Spoon salmon mixture into dish; top with mash, sprinkle with parmesan. Bake about 20 minutes or until top is golden. Place under a hot grill for 5 minutes or until browned. Serve topped with extra dill.

potato and celeriac mash Boil, steam or microwave potato and celeriac, separately, until tender; drain. Mash potato and celeriac in a large bowl with milk and butter until smooth. Stir in parmesan; season to taste.

tip Recipe can be made in two 1-litre (4-cup) ovenproof dishes as shown in image.

Fetta, basil & vegetable
LAMB ROASTS

PREP & COOK TIME 50 MINUTES **SERVES** 6

½ cup (100g) drained char-grilled vegetables, chopped coarsely

50g (1½ ounces) fetta, crumbled

2 tablespoons coarsely chopped fresh basil

4 lamb mini roasts (1.4kg)

1kg (2 pounds) kumara (orange sweet potato), cut into wedges

cooking-oil spray

1 tablespoon coarsely chopped fresh rosemary

1 Preheat oven to 220°C/425°F.

2 Combine char-grilled vegetables, fetta and basil in a small bowl.

3 Make a horizontal cut in each lamb roast to make a large pocket, without cutting all the way through. Push vegetable mixture into pockets. Tie lamb at 3cm (1¼-inch) intervals with kitchen string. Place lamb on a large oiled oven tray. Add kumara to tray; spray with oil, season.

4 Roast lamb and kumara, uncovered, about 35 minutes. Cover lamb; stand 10 minutes. Remove kitchen string, then slice thickly.

serving suggestion Serve with a rocket (arugula) and mixed tomato salad.

Healthy CHOICE

Kid FRIENDLY

Little cottage pies
WITH CHEESY MASH

PREP & COOK TIME 50 MINUTES SERVES 6

2 teaspoons vegetable oil

1 medium brown onion (150g), chopped finely

2 cloves garlic, crushed

750g (1½ pounds) minced (ground) beef

2 stalks celery (300g), trimmed, chopped finely

¼ cup (35g) plain (all-purpose) flour

1 cup (250ml) beef stock

2 tablespoons worcestershire sauce

1½ cups (180g) frozen peas

2 x 600g (1¼-pound) tubs prepared mashed potato

½ cup (40g) finely grated parmesan

1 Preheat oven to 200°C/400°F.

2 Meanwhile, heat oil in a large saucepan over medium-high heat, add onion, garlic and beef; cook, stirring, until browned. Add celery; cook, stirring, until soft. Stir in flour then gradually add stock and sauce; cook, stirring, until mixture boils and thickens. Stir in peas; season.

3 Spoon mixture into six 1¾-cup (430ml) ovenproof dishes; top with mash, sprinkle with parmesan.

4 Bake pies about 20 minutes or until heated through. Place under a hot grill for 5 minutes or until browned.

serving suggestion Serve with a rocket (arugula), flat-leaf parsley and red onion salad.

tips This pie is suitable to freeze. Thaw in the fridge overnight before reheating.

Fried rice OMELETTE

PREP & COOK TIME 15 MINUTES
SERVES 4

Cut 1 large carrot and 1 medium red capsicum (bell pepper) into thin matchsticks. Heat 500g (1lb) packaged microwave fried rice in a microwave according to directions on packet. Meanwhile, lightly beat 10 eggs and 2 tablespoons water in a large bowl until combined; season. Heat an oiled medium frying pan over high heat. Cook one-quarter of the egg mixture about 1 minute or until starting to set. Spoon a quarter of the hot rice along centre of omelette; top with one-quarter of the carrot and capsicum. Fold omelette into three; slide onto a warm plate. Repeat with remaining egg mixture, rice and vegetables to make 4 omelettes. Sprinkle with 1 cup fresh coriander (cilantro) sprigs and 1 thinly sliced fresh long red chilli. Serve with chilli sauce and lime wedges, if you like.

Cheat's BIRYANI

PREP & COOK TIME 15 MINUTES
SERVES 4

Heat ¼ cup (60g) ghee in a large saucepan over medium-high heat; cook 1 thinly sliced medium brown onion and 2 teaspoons garam masala, stirring, about 2 minutes or until onion is softened and browned lightly. Add 500g (1lb) coarsely chopped lamb stir-fry strips; cook, stirring, about 2 minutes or until browned. Meanwhile, heat 450g (14½oz) packaged microwave basmati rice according to directions on packet. Remove lamb mixture from heat; stir in rice and ⅓ cup (50g) raisins. Season to taste. Sprinkle biryani with ⅓ cup loosely packed fresh coriander (cilantro) leaves and 2 tablespoons roasted flaked almonds; serve immediately, accompanied with yoghurt and pappadams.

tip Use olive oil instead of ghee, if you like.

Broccoli, blue cheese
& RICE FRITTATA
PREP & COOK TIME 25 MINUTES
SERVES 6

Boil, steam or microwave 1 cup small broccoli florets until
tender; drain. Heat 250g (8oz) packaged microwave white
long-grain rice according to directions on packet. Combine
rice with broccoli, ½ cup coarsely chopped drained char-
grilled capsicum (bell pepper), 8 lightly beaten eggs, 60g
(2oz) crumbled mild blue cheese, ¼ cup coarsely chopped
fresh flat-leaf parsley and ¼ cup (60ml) cold water in a large
bowl; season. Pour mixture evenly into two heated oiled frying
pans with heatproof handles (base measures 15cm/6in);
cover loosely with foil, cook over low heat 15 minutes.
Preheat grill (broiler). Uncover frittatas; cook under grill
about 5 minutes or until set and browned lightly. Stand
5 minutes before serving topped with extra 30g (1oz)
crumbled blue cheese and fresh flat-leaf parsley leaves.

Cheesy prosciutto
RICE CAKES
PREP & COOK TIME 15 MINUTES
SERVES 4

Heat 450g (14½oz) packaged microwave white long-grain
rice according to directions on packet. Place ½ cup (60g)
frozen peas in a small heatproof bowl, cover with boiling
water. Stand 1 minute, then drain. Combine peas, rice,
2 coarsely chopped slices prosciutto (30g), 2 teaspoons
finely grated lemon rind, ¼ cup finely chopped fresh
chives, 1½ cups (150g) coarsely grated mozzarella, 2 eggs
and ½ cup (50g) packaged breadcrumbs in a large bowl;
season. Heat an oiled large frying pan over medium heat.
Using wet hands, shape ¼-cups of rice mixture into patties.
Cook patties, in batches, about 2 minutes each side or until
browned and cooked through. Repeat to make a total of
12 patties. Serve patties with watercress; accompany with
tomato relish.

EXPRESS
PASTA

Fettuccine with chicken, PEAR & BLUE CHEESE

PREP & COOK TIME 30 MINUTES   SERVES 4

500g (1 pound) fettuccine

½ cup (50g) walnuts

50g (1½ ounces) butter

2 baby pears (200g), sliced thinly

1 clove garlic, crushed

2½ cups (400g) shredded cooked chicken

1 cup (250ml) pouring cream

1 medium radicchio (200g), leaves separated, torn

80g (2½ ounces) blue cheese, crumbled

⅓ cup loosely packed fresh flat-leaf parsley leaves

1 Cook pasta in a large saucepan of boiling salted water about 8 minutes or until just tender; drain. Return to pan to keep warm.

2 Meanwhile, toast walnuts in a large frying pan over medium heat for 5 minutes or until browned lightly. Chop coarsely.

3 Melt butter in same frying pan over medium-high heat; cook pear, stirring, 2 minutes or until beginning to caramelise. Add garlic; cook, stirring, until fragrant. Stir in chicken and cream; bring to the boil.

4 Add pasta, radicchio and half the nuts to pear mixture, sprinkle with cheese; toss gently to combine. Season to taste. Serve sprinkled with remaining nuts and parsley.

tip We used corella pears.

Pork, sopressa & KALE PESTO PASTA

PREP & COOK TIME 30 MINUTES SERVES 4

½ cup (125ml) olive oil

600g (1¼ pounds) pork fillets

375g (12 ounces) casarecci pasta

1 medium brown onion (150g), chopped finely

2 cloves garlic, crushed

100g (3 ounces) hot sopressa salami, sliced thinly

100g (3 ounces) baby kale leaves

¼ cup (20g) finely grated parmesan

1 tablespoon roasted pine nuts

2 tablespoons lemon juice

½ cup micro basil leaves

1 Heat 1 tablespoon of the oil in a large frying pan over medium-high heat; cook pork, turning, about 15 minutes or until cooked. Remove from pan; cover to keep warm.

2 Meanwhile, cook pasta in a large saucepan of boiling salted water about 8 minutes or until tender; drain. Return to pan to keep warm.

3 Cook onion, garlic and salami in same frying pan, stirring, about 5 minutes or until onion softens.

4 Blend or process kale, remaining oil, parmesan, nuts and juice until smooth; season to taste.

5 Thinly slice pork. Add pork, salami mixture and kale pesto to pasta in pan; toss to combine. Serve sprinkled with basil leaves.

tip Sopressa, a salami from the north of Italy, can be found in both mild and chilli-flavoured varieties. If unavailable, you can use any hot salami.

Pea, semi-dried tomato & BOCCONCINI PASTA

PREP & COOK TIME 15 MINUTES SERVES 4

375g (12 ounces) penne pasta

1 cup (120g) frozen peas

340g (11 ounces) bottled semi-dried tomatoes in oil

4 bocconcini (240g), torn

⅓ cup loosely packed fresh small basil leaves

1 Cook pasta in a large saucepan of boiling salted water about 8 minutes or until tender. Add peas, return to the boil. Drain.

2 Meanwhile, drain tomatoes, reserve 2 tablespoons of the oil.

3 Return pasta and peas to pan with tomatoes, reserved oil and bocconcini; stir gently to combine. Season to taste. Serve topped with basil and cracked black pepper.

Chilli squid spaghetti
WITH ZESTY ROCKET PESTO

PREP & COOK TIME 30 MINUTES   **SERVES** 4

500g (1 pound) cleaned squid hoods

2 medium lemons (280g)

500g (1 pound) spaghetti

½ cup (75g) roasted unsalted cashews

⅓ cup (50g) roasted pine nuts

1 cup firmly packed fresh basil leaves

50g (1½ ounces) rocket (arugula)

1 teaspoon sea salt flakes

1¼ cups (100g) finely grated parmesan

1¼ cups (300ml) extra virgin olive oil

1 fresh long red chilli, chopped finely

60g (2 ounces) rocket (arugula), extra

¼ cup firmly packed fresh small basil leaves, extra

1 Open squid out flat; score inside diagonally, in a criss-cross pattern, at 1cm (½-inch) intervals. Cut squid into thick strips.

2 Finely grate rind from one lemon. Remove rind from remaining lemon with a zester (or cut rind into thin strips avoiding the white pith). Squeeze juice from lemons; you will need ¼ cup.

3 Cook spaghetti in a large saucepan of boiling salted water for 8 minutes or until just tender; drain. Return to pan to keep warm.

4 Meanwhile, to make pesto, blend or process nuts, basil, rocket, lemon juice, salt, 1 cup of the parmesan and 1 cup of the oil until almost smooth. Season to taste.

5 Heat remaining oil in a large deep frying pan over high heat; cook squid, in batches, for 2 minutes or until tender and opaque. Add pesto to squid with pasta, half the chilli and grated rind; toss until heated through.

6 Serve spaghetti sprinkled with extra rocket, remaining parmesan and chilli, strips of rind and extra basil leaves.

tips You can use spaghettini or linguine for this recipe. The lemon juice in the pesto will discolour it quickly so use it immediately. If you wish to make it ahead without the juice, keep it covered tightly, then stir in the lemon juice just before serving.

Creamy chilli & GARLIC PRAWN FETTUCCINE

PREP & COOK TIME 30 MINUTES SERVES 4

375g (12 ounces) curly fettuccine

300g (9½ ounces) brussels sprouts

1kg (2 pounds) uncooked medium prawns (shrimp)

4 cloves garlic, crushed

2 fresh small red thai chillies, chopped finely

2 tablespoons olive oil

½ cup (125ml) chicken stock

300ml pouring cream

1 tablespoon lemon juice

1 tablespoon finely chopped fresh flat-leaf parsley

1 Cook pasta in a large saucepan of boiling salted water about 8 minutes or until tender; drain. Return to pan to keep warm.

2 Meanwhile, reserve outer leaves from brussels sprouts; halve sprouts. Peel and devein prawns, leaving tails intact. Combine prawns, garlic and chilli in a medium bowl.

3 Heat half the oil in a large deep frying pan; cook prawns, stirring, until changed in colour. Remove from pan.

4 Heat remaining oil in same pan; cook halved sprouts, stirring, until browned lightly. Return prawns to pan with stock, cream and juice; bring to the boil. Reduce heat; simmer, uncovered, about 5 minutes or until sauce thickens slightly. Add pasta, parsley and reserved brussels sprout leaves; toss until heated through. Season to taste.

tips To save time, you can buy 250g (8 ounces) shelled prawns from the fishmonger or you can find them in the freezer section in most large supermarkets. Omit the chilli if you don't like it spicy.

Meat FREE

Pappardelle with ricotta, CAPSICUM & CAVOLO NERO

PREP & COOK TIME 35 MINUTES SERVES 4

¼ cup (60ml) olive oil

2 cloves garlic, crushed

½ teaspoon dried chilli flakes

4 large red capsicums (bell peppers) (1.5kg), sliced thinly

¼ cup (60ml) water

200g (6½ ounces) cavolo nero (tuscan cabbage), trimmed, shredded coarsely

375g (12 ounces) pappardelle pasta

¼ cup finely chopped fresh chives

2 cups (400g) firm ricotta

½ cup (100g) firm ricotta, extra, crumbled

1 Heat oil in a large saucepan over medium-high heat; cook garlic and chilli, stirring, for 1 minutes or until fragrant. Add capsicum and the water; simmer, covered, for 5 minutes. Add cavolo nero; simmer, covered, about 5 minutes or until capsicum is soft and cavolo nero is tender.

2 Meanwhile, cook pasta in a large saucepan of boiling salted water about 8 minutes or until tender; drain.

3 Add pasta and chives to capsicum mixture. Break ricotta into large pieces, add to pan; toss gently. Season to taste.

4 Serve pasta topped with extra ricotta. If you like, sprinkle with extra dried chilli and drizzle with a little extra olive oil before serving.

One pot
SPAGHETTI MARINARA

PREP & COOK TIME 25 MINUTES SERVES 4

1 tablespoon olive oil

1 medium brown onion (150g), chopped finely

2 cloves garlic, crushed

1 fresh long red chilli, chopped finely

400g (12½ ounces) canned diced tomatoes

⅓ cup coarsely chopped fresh basil

1 litre (4 cups) water

500g (1 pound) spaghetti

500g (1 pound) marinara mix

2 tablespoons olive oil, extra

⅓ cup small fresh basil leaves

1 Heat oil in a large saucepan; cook onion, garlic and chilli, stirring, until onion softens. Add tomatoes and chopped basil; cook, stirring, 1 minute.

2 Add the water to the pan; bring to the boil. Add pasta; once pasta begins to soften, gently mix into the tomato mixture. Boil, uncovered, stirring, for 5 minutes. Add marinara mix; boil, uncovered, stirring, for about 5 minutes or until pasta is tender and seafood is just cooked. Season to taste.

3 Serve bowls of pasta drizzled with extra oil and sprinkled with basil leaves.

tips This recipe is quite versatile – here we used marinara mix but you could easily change this basic sauce recipe to suit your tastes and needs. You could use the same amount of shelled uncooked prawns or shredded barbecued chicken. For a vegetarian option, instead of the marinara mix try adding some char-grilled eggplant or marinated antipasto vegetables and fresh rocket at the end of step 2. Another variation is to cook some thinly sliced bacon with the onion mixture in step 1 to make spaghetti amatriciana.

One
PAN

Prawn & fennel
SPAGHETTINI

PREP & COOK TIME 20 MINUTES SERVES 4

375g (12 ounces) spaghettini pasta

2 tablespoons olive oil

500g (1 pound) uncooked shelled medium king prawns (shrimp)

2 fresh long red chillies, chopped finely

2 baby fennel bulbs (260g), sliced thinly, fronds reserved

2 cloves garlic, crushed

1 tablespoon finely grated lemon rind

2 tablespoons lemon juice

100g (3 ounces) baby rocket (arugula) leaves

1 Cook pasta in a large saucepan of boiling salted water about 8 minutes or until tender; drain, reserving 1 cup (250ml) cooking liquid.

2 Meanwhile, heat oil in a large deep frying pan over high heat; cook prawns, chilli, fennel and garlic, stirring, for 2 minutes. Stir in reserved cooking liquid from pasta, rind and juice; remove from heat. Add pasta and rocket; toss to combine, season to taste.

3 Serve pasta sprinkled with reserved fennel fronds.

Farfalle with zucchini, SPINACH & LEMON

Meat FREE

Farfalle with zucchini, SPINACH & LEMON

PREP & COOK TIME 30 MINUTES   SERVES 4

375g (12 ounces) farfalle pasta

6 medium green zucchini (560g)

30g (1 ounce) butter

1 tablespoon olive oil

2 cloves garlic, crushed

¼ cup (60ml) dry white wine

⅓ cup (80ml) vegetable stock

½ cup (125ml) pouring cream

2 teaspoons finely grated lemon rind

75g (2½ ounces) baby spinach leaves

⅓ cup coarsely chopped fresh chives

¼ cup (20g) flaked parmesan

1 Cook pasta in a large saucepan of boiling salted water until just tender; drain. Return to pan.
2 Meanwhile, cut zucchini in half lengthways; slice thinly on the diagonal.
3 Heat butter and oil in a large deep frying pan over high heat; cook zucchini and garlic, stirring, for 8 minutes or until zucchini is just tender. Add wine and stock; bring to the boil. Reduce heat; stir in cream, rind, spinach and chives until hot.
4 Add pasta to zucchini mixture, season; toss to combine. Serve topped with parmesan.

serving suggestion Serve with a multi-coloured tomato salad tossed in a balsamic dressing.

Spaghettini NIÇOISE

PREP & COOK TIME 30 MINUTES   SERVES 4

250g (8 ounces) spaghettini pasta

4 eggs

425g (13½ ounces) canned tuna chunks in olive oil, drained, flaked

⅓ cup (55g) seeded kalamata olives, chopped coarsely

250g (8 ounces) cherry tomatoes, halved

⅓ cup (50g) roasted pine nuts

100g (3 ounces) baby rocket (arugula) leaves

½ teaspoon dried chilli flakes

lemon mustard dressing

2 tablespoons olive oil

1 tablespoon finely grated lemon rind

¼ cup (60ml) lemon juice

1 clove garlic, crushed

1 tablespoon dijon mustard

1 tablespoon rinsed, drained baby capers

1 Make lemon mustard dressing.

2 Cook pasta in a large saucepan of boiling salted water about 8 minutes or until tender; drain. Return to pan to keep warm.

3 Meanwhile, place eggs in a small saucepan, cover with cold water; bring to the boil. Boil, uncovered, for 2 minutes or until soft-boiled. Drain; rinse under cold water. When cool enough to handle, peel eggs.

4 Add tuna, olives, tomatoes, nuts, rocket and dressing to pasta in pan; toss gently. Season to taste. Serve pasta topped with halved soft-boiled eggs and chilli flakes.

lemon mustard dressing Place ingredients in a screw-top jar; shake well.

Cheap
EAT

Rigatoni with eggplant & ITALIAN SAUSAGE

PREP & COOK TIME 30 MINUTES SERVES 4

6 italian-style pork and fennel sausages (720g)

¼ cup (60ml) olive oil

1 medium onion (150g), chopped finely

2 stalks celery (300g), trimmed, chopped finely

1 clove garlic, crushed

2 tablespoons brandy (optional)

1 medium eggplant (300g), chopped coarsely

2⅓ cups (600g) bottled passata

½ cup (140g) tomato paste

½ cup (125ml) water

375g (12 ounces) rigatoni pasta

2 tablespoons fresh basil leaves

¼ cup (20g) shaved parmesan

1 Squeeze sausage meat from casings into a medium bowl; discard casings. Coarsely crumble sausage meat.

2 Heat a large saucepan over high heat; cook sausage meat, stirring, about 8 minutes or until browned. Remove from pan; drain on paper towel.

3 Add oil to same pan and reduce heat to medium-high; cook onion, celery and garlic, stirring, about 5 minutes or until onion softens. Add brandy; cook, stirring, until brandy evaporates. Add eggplant; cook, stirring, until tender.

4 Return sausage meat to pan with sauce, paste and the water; bring to the boil. Reduce heat; simmer, uncovered, about 10 minutes or until sauce thickens slightly. Season to taste.

5 Meanwhile, cook pasta in a large saucepan of boiling salted water about 10 minutes or until tender; drain. Return to pan to keep warm.

6 Add sauce to pasta in pan; toss to combine. Serve topped with basil and parmesan.

Casarecci with artichokes
& LEMON GARLIC CRUMBS

PREP & COOK TIME 30 MINUTES   SERVES 4

500g (1 pound) casarecci pasta

⅓ cup (80ml) olive oil

1 clove garlic, crushed

400g (12½ ounces) canned artichoke hearts, drained, halved

¾ cup (180g) firm ricotta, crumbled

¼ cup loosely packed fresh small mint leaves

¼ cup loosely packed fresh flat-leaf parsley leaves

parsley oil

1 cup firmly packed fresh flat-leaf parsley leaves

½ cup (125ml) olive oil

1 tablespoon lemon juice

lemon and garlic crumbs

40g (1½ ounces) butter

1 tablespoon olive oil

1 clove garlic, crushed

1 teaspoon finely grated lemon rind

1 cup (70g) coarse fresh breadcrumbs

1 Cook pasta in a large saucepan of boiling salted water about 8 minutes or until tender; drain. Return pasta to pan to keep warm.

2 Meanwhile, make parsley oil. Make lemon and garlic crumbs.

3 Heat oil in a large deep frying pan over medium-high heat; cook garlic and artichokes, stirring, about 2 minutes or until heated through. Add pasta to pan with ricotta and herbs; toss to combine. Season to taste.

4 Serve topped with lemon and garlic crumbs, drizzle with parsley oil.

parsley oil Blend or process ingredients until smooth.

lemon and garlic crumbs Heat butter and oil in a medium frying pan over medium heat; cook garlic, rind and breadcrumbs, stirring, until breadcrumbs are golden and crisp. Remove from pan.

Chicken ravioli with TARRAGON SAUCE

PREP & COOK TIME 40 MINUTES **SERVES** 4

350g (11 ounces) minced (ground) chicken

1 green onion (scallion), sliced thinly

2 teaspoons finely grated lemon rind

28 gow gee wrappers

1 egg, beaten lightly

2 teaspoons olive oil

1 medium brown onion (150g), chopped finely

1 clove garlic, crushed

⅓ cup (80ml) dry white wine

2 teaspoons dijon mustard

300ml pouring cream

1 tablespoon finely shredded fresh tarragon

1 Combine chicken, green onion and rind in a medium bowl; season.

2 Brush one wrapper at a time with egg. Place a rounded teaspoon of the chicken mixture in the centre of wrapper. Fold over to enclose filling; press edge to seal. Repeat to make a total of 28 ravioli. Place ravioli, in a single layer, on tray.

3 Heat oil in a medium saucepan over medium-high heat; cook brown onion and garlic, stirring, about 5 minutes or until onion softens. Add wine; cook, stirring, about 5 minutes or until wine reduces by half. Stir in mustard and cream; cook sauce, stirring, until mixture just boils.

4 Meanwhile, cook pasta in a large saucepan of boiling water until pasta floats to the top; drain. Add pasta and tarragon to cream sauce. Toss gently until pasta is warmed through. Serve topped with extra fresh tarragon, if you like.

Chicken, mushroom, pea & PROSCIUTTO PASTA

PREP & COOK TIME 40 MINUTES SERVES 6

6 slices prosciutto (90g)

500g (1 pound) spiral pasta

2 tablespoons garlic butter spread

200g (6½ ounces) thinly sliced swiss brown mushrooms

3 cups (480g) shredded barbecued chicken

150g (4½ ounces) sugar snap peas, trimmed, halved lengthways

200g (6½ ounces) danish fetta, crumbled

300ml pouring cream

2 tablespoons coarsely chopped fresh tarragon

½ cup loosely packed lamb's tongue leaves

1 Preheat grill (broiler).

2 Place prosciutto on an oven tray; grill about 3 minutes or until prosciutto is crisp. Drain on paper towel.

3 Cook pasta in a large saucepan of boiling salted water about 8 minutes or until tender. Drain, reserving 2 cups of the cooking liquid. Wipe saucepan clean.

4 Melt butter in cleaned pan; cook mushrooms, over medium heat, stirring until golden and tender.

5 Return pasta to pan; add chicken and peas. Stir in fetta, cream, tarragon and reserved cooking liquid; cook, stirring until creamy and heated through. Season to taste.

6 Serve pasta topped with crumbled prosciutto and lamb's tongue.

tips You will need a barbecued chicken weighing about 900g (1¾ pounds) for this recipe. You can use baby cress instead of lamb's tongue, if you prefer.

Wholemeal spaghetti with
MUSHROOMS & ALMONDS

PREP & COOK TIME 35 MINUTES SERVES 4

375g (12 ounces) wholegrain spaghetti

2 tablespoons olive oil

400g (12½ ounces) swiss brown mushrooms, sliced

400g (12½ ounces) portobello mushrooms, sliced

2 shallots (25g), chopped coarsely

2 cloves garlic, chopped coarsely

½ cup (80g) coarsely chopped roasted almonds

150g (4½ ounces) baby spinach leaves

½ cup (40g) finely grated pecorino cheese

¼ cup loosely packed fresh flat-leaf parsley leaves

1 Cook pasta in a large saucepan of boiling water about 10 minutes or until tender; drain, reserving 1 cup (250ml) of the cooking liquid.

2 Meanwhile, heat oil in a large deep frying pan over high heat; cook mushrooms and shallot, stirring occasionally, for 5 minutes or until mushrooms are lightly golden and shallot is tender. Add garlic; cook, stirring, for 1 minute or until fragrant. Season to taste.

3 Reduce heat to low; toss warm pasta, nuts and spinach through mushroom mixture. Add enough reserved pasta water to lightly coat the pasta. Serve topped with cheese and parsley.

tips You can use 800g (1¼ pounds) of your favourite variety of mushrooms; button and cap mushrooms will work well. If you don't have a large frying pan, cook the mushrooms in batches to prevent them stewing.

Linguine with
SILVER BEET & PANCETTA

PREP & COOK TIME 35 MINUTES SERVES 4

375g (12 ounces) linguine

⅓ cup (80ml) olive oil

2 cloves garlic, crushed

1 small brown onion (80g), chopped finely

90g (3 ounces) hot pancetta, sliced thinly

2 medium silver beet (swiss chard) leaves (130g), trimmed, chopped coarsely

½ cup (40g) finely grated parmesan

1 Cook pasta in a large saucepan of boiling salted water about 8 minutes until tender; drain. Return to pan to keep warm.

2 Meanwhile, heat oil in a large deep frying pan over medium-high heat; cook garlic, onion and pancetta, stirring, about 5 minutes or until onion softens and pancetta is browned. Add silver beet; cook, stirring, until wilted.

3 Add pasta and parmesan to pan; toss to combine. Season to taste.

Spaghetti & eggplant 'MEATBALLS'

PREP & COOK TIME 1 HOUR SERVES 6

1 medium eggplant (300g), peeled, chopped coarsely

2 tablespoons olive oil

400g (12½ ounces) canned chickpeas (garbanzo beans), drained, rinsed

1 small red onion (100g), chopped finely

2 cloves garlic, crushed

1 tablespoon finely chopped fresh rosemary leaves

1 cup (80g) finely grated parmesan

1½ cups (150g) packaged breadcrumbs

vegetable oil, for shallow-frying

375g (12 ounces) spaghetti

700g (1½ pounds) bottled tomato pasta sauce

⅓ cup (25g) finely grated parmesan, extra

2 tablespoons small basil leaves

1 Preheat oven to 200°C/400°F. Line an oven tray with baking paper.

2 Place eggplant on tray; drizzle with olive oil. Roast for 25 minutes or until golden and tender.

3 Process eggplant, chickpeas, onion, garlic, rosemary and parmesan until combined; season. Add 1 cup breadcrumbs; pulse until combined. Roll level tablespoons of eggplant mixture into 24 balls. Roll eggplant balls in remaining breadcrumbs to coat.

4 Heat vegetable oil in a large frying pan; shallow-fry eggplant balls, in batches, about 2 minutes or until golden and heated through. Drain on paper towel.

5 Meanwhile, cook pasta in a large saucepan of boiling salted water about 8 minutes or until tender; drain. Return to pan to keep warm.

6 Bring sauce to the boil in a large frying pan; add eggplant balls, simmer, uncovered, until heated through. Season.

7 Serve pasta topped with eggplant balls and sauce; sprinkle with extra parmesan and basil.

Spicy zucchini & RICOTTA PASTA SHELLS

PREP & COOK TIME 1 HOUR   SERVES 4

3 medium zucchini (360g)

1⅓ cups (320g) firm ricotta

¾ cup (60g) finely grated parmesan

⅓ cup (50g) roasted pine nuts

3 egg yolks

2 cloves garlic, crushed

1 tablespoon fresh lemon thyme leaves

½ teaspoon dried chilli flakes

5 cups (1.3kg) bottled tomato pasta sauce

250g (8 ounces) large pasta shells

1 tablespoon fresh lemon thyme leaves, extra

1 Preheat oven to 200°C/400°F. Oil a shallow 2.5-litre (10-cup) ovenproof dish.

2 Coarsely grate zucchini. Combine zucchini, ricotta, parmesan, nuts, egg yolks, garlic, lemon thyme and chilli in a medium bowl; season.

3 Spread pasta sauce into dish; season. Spoon zucchini mixture into uncooked pasta shells; place in dish.

4 Cover dish with foil; bake 30 minutes. Uncover; bake about 15 minutes or until pasta is tender and cheese is browned lightly. Serve pasta sprinkled with extra lemon thyme leaves.

serving suggestion Serve with a green salad.

One
PAN

Seafood risoni PAELLA

PREP & COOK TIME 1 HOUR SERVES 4

2 tablespoons olive oil

1 small brown onion (80g), chopped finely

4 cloves garlic, crushed

500g (1 pound) risoni pasta

pinch saffron threads

1 cup (250ml) dry white wine

6 small tomatoes (540g), seeded, chopped coarsely

2 tablespoons tomato paste

1 teaspoon finely grated orange rind

4 sprigs fresh marjoram

1 litre (4 cups) chicken stock, warmed

1½ cups (180g) frozen peas

⅓ cup (80g) finely chopped drained char-grilled capsicum (bell pepper)

500g (1 pound) pot-ready mussels

4 large uncooked king prawns (shrimp) (280g), peeled, deveined, leaving heads and tails intact

1 large cleaned squid hood (150g), cut into 1cm (½-inch) thick rings

⅓ cup coarsely chopped fresh flat-leaf parsley

1 medium lemon (140g), cut into wedges

1 Heat oil in a large deep frying pan over medium-high heat; cook onion and garlic, stirring, about 5 minutes or until onion softens. Add pasta and saffron; stir to coat in onion mixture. Stir in wine, tomatoes, paste, rind and marjoram; cook, stirring, until wine has almost evaporated.

2 Add 1 cup of the stock; stir until liquid is absorbed. Add remaining stock; cook, stirring, about 8 minutes or until pasta is almost tender. Season to taste.

3 Place peas, capsicum and seafood on top of risoni mixture; do not stir to combine. Cover pan, reduce heat; simmer about 10 minutes or until seafood has changed in colour and mussels have opened. Sprinkle with parsley; serve with lemon wedges.

tips You can use 750g (1½ pounds) uncooked marinara seafood mix instead of the mussels, prawns and squid. This recipe can be made in a traditional paella pan if you own one, otherwise a deep frying pan or wok with a tight-fitting lid will suffice. Serve the paella straight from the pan at the table.

FAST GNOCCHI

Gnocchi with KUMARA & PINE NUTS

PREP & COOK TIME 30 MINUTES
SERVES 6

Preheat oven to 200°C/400°F. Chop 800g (1½lb) kumara (orange sweet potato) into 1cm (½-inch) pieces. Combine kumara and 1 tablespoon olive oil in a shallow medium baking dish, season; roast about 20 minutes or until tender. Meanwhile, cook 500g (1lb) potato gnocchi in a large saucepan of boiling salted water until gnocchi float to the surface; drain. Melt 150g (4½oz) butter in a medium frying pan with 1 tablespoon olive oil; cook 3 finely chopped medium tomatoes and ¾ cup loosely packed fresh sage leaves, stirring, for 2 minutes or until tomato softens slightly and butter is browned lightly. Combine gnocchi, kumara, tomato mixture, 60g (2oz) baby spinach leaves, ½ cup (40g) flaked parmesan and ⅓ cup (50g) roasted pine nuts in a large bowl. Season to taste.

Mixed mushroom GNOCCHI BOSCAIOLA

PREP & COOK TIME 40 MINUTES
SERVES 6

Combine 10g (½oz) dried porcini mushrooms and ¼ cup (60ml) boiling water in a small heatproof bowl; cover, stand for 15 minutes or until tender. Drain; reserve soaking liquid, chop mushrooms coarsely. Meanwhile, cook 500g (1lb) potato gnocchi in a large saucepan of boiling salted water until gnocchi float to the surface; drain. Cook 200g (6½oz) chopped pancetta in a heated oiled large deep frying pan until crisp. Add 300g (10oz) thinly sliced mixed mushrooms and 2 crushed garlic cloves; cook, stirring, until mushrooms are browned lightly. Add 300ml pouring cream, 1 tablespoon lemon juice and the porcini mushrooms and reserved liquid; simmer, uncovered, until sauce reduces by half and thickens slightly. Stir in gnocchi, ½ cup (40g) finely grated parmesan and 2 tablespoons chopped fresh chives. Season.

Gnocchi with pork,
FENNEL & TOMATO
PREP & COOK TIME 25 MINUTES
SERVES 6

Cook 1.2kg (2½lb) italian-style pork and fennel sausages in a heated oiled large deep frying pan. Remove from pan, slice thickly; cover to keep warm. Add 6 coarsely chopped medium tomatoes (900g) to pan; bring to the boil. Reduce heat; simmer, uncovered, about 2 minutes or until thickened slightly. Season to taste. Meanwhile, cook 500g (1lb) potato gnocchi in a large saucepan of boiling salted water until gnocchi float to the surface; drain. Return sausages to tomato mixture in pan with gnocchi and 100g (3oz) baby rocket (arugula) leaves; toss to combine. Season to taste. Serve topped with ⅓ cup (25g) flaked parmesan.

Lamb cutlets with
PESTO GNOCCHI
PREP & COOK TIME 25 MINUTES
SERVES 4

Cook 250g (8oz) potato gnocchi in a large saucepan of boiling salted water until gnocchi floats to the surface; drain. Heat 1 tablespoon oil in a large frying pan over medium heat; cook 12 french-trimmed lamb cutlets (600g), about 2 minutes each side or until browned and cooked as desired. Remove from pan, cover; stand for 5 minutes. Add ½ cup (125ml) dry white wine to same pan; bring to the boil. Reduce heat; simmer until the wine has reduced by about one third. Stir in ½ cup (130g) basil pesto and ⅓ cup (80ml) pouring cream; simmer until sauce thickens slightly. Add gnocchi; stir until heated through. Season to taste. Serve lamb with gnocchi, sprinkle with ¼ cup firmly packed fresh small basil leaves.

EXPRESS GRILLS & PAN-FRIES

Pork
PARMIGIANA BAKE

PREP & COOK TIME 25 MINUTES SERVES 4

1 small eggplant (230g), sliced thinly lengthways

cooking-oil spray

4 slices prosciutto (60g)

2 tablespoons olive oil

4 uncrumbed pork schnitzels (800g)

4 bocconcini (100g)

400g (12½ ounces) canned cherry tomatoes

⅓ cup loosely packed fresh cress or baby basil leaves

1 Spray eggplant on both sides with cooking oil; cook on a heated grill plate (or grill or barbecue) over high heat, for 2 minutes each side or until browned and tender.

2 Meanwhile, preheat grill (broiler). Place prosciutto on a baking-paper-lined oven tray; place under grill. Grill about 3 minutes or until prosciutto is browned and crisp. Remove from grill; cover to keep warm. Leave grill on.

3 Meanwhile, heat half the oil in a shallow 2-litre (8-cup) flameproof baking dish over medium-high heat on stove top. Season pork; cook about 1 minute each side or until almost cooked through, remove from heat. Remove pork from dish.

4 Slice bocconcini thinly. Add tomatoes to dish; place pork on top. Top pork with eggplant and bocconcini.

5 Place baking dish under grill; cook about 3 minutes or until bocconcini melts and pork is cooked through.

6 To serve, spoon tomato over the pork stacks, top with prosciutto and cress; drizzle with remaining oil.

tips Put the baking dish as close to the preheated grill as possible. This dish can be served as is, or accompany it with a salad, or mashed potato and fresh crusty bread to soak up the juices.

Margarita FISH

PREP & COOK TIME 15 MINUTES SERVES 4

1 lime

4 x 200g (6½-ounce) firm white fish fillets

1 teaspoon dried chilli flakes

1 clove garlic, crushed

2 tablespoons olive oil

500g (1 pound) cherry truss tomatoes

2 tablespoons tequila

2 tablespoons olive oil, extra

1 tablespoon caster (superfine) sugar

450g (14½ ounces) package microwave white long-grain rice

2 cups loosely packed fresh coriander (cilantro) leaves

1 Heat an oiled grill plate (or grill or barbecue). Preheat grill (broiler).

2 Cut lime rind into thin strips; squeeze juice from lime. Combine rind, fish, chilli, garlic and oil in a large bowl; season. Cook fish on grill plate about 3 minutes each side or until cooked through.

3 Meanwhile, grill tomatoes until just beginning to split.

4 Combine juice, tequila, extra oil and sugar in a medium bowl; season to taste.

5 Microwave rice according to directions on packet.

6 Serve fish with rice; top with tomatoes, coriander and tequila mixture. Accompany with lime wedges, if you like.

serving suggestion Serve with a green leafy salad.

tip We used coral trout for this recipe but you can use any firm white fish fillets you like.

Sandwich press
CHICKEN QUESADILLAS

PREP & COOK TIME 25 MINUTES SERVES 4

1 medium avocado (250g), chopped coarsely

1 cup loosely packed fresh coriander (cilantro) leaves

1 tablespoon lemon juice

1 tablespoon vegetable oil

500g (1 pound) minced (ground) chicken

2 teaspoons ground cumin

400g (12½ ounces) canned kidney beans, drained, rinsed

3 medium roma (egg) tomatoes (225g), chopped finely

3 green onions (scallions), sliced thinly

8 x 19cm (7¾-inch) flour tortillas

1 cup (120g) grated cheddar

1 medium lemon (140g), cut into wedges

1 Combine avocado, coriander and juice in a small bowl. Season to taste.

2 Heat oil in a large frying pan; cook the chicken, stirring, until browned. Add cumin; cook, stirring, 1 minute or until fragrant. Stir in the beans, tomato and onion. Remove pan from heat.

3 Divide chicken mixture among four tortillas; sprinkle with cheese. Top with remaining tortillas. Cook one at a time in a preheated sandwich press, for about 2 minutes or until cheddar is melted and tortillas are browned lightly.

4 Cut quesadillas into quarters; serve with avocado mixture and lemon wedges.

serving suggestion Serve with sour cream and a baby leaf and cucumber salad.

tip If you don't have a sandwich press, cook these in a large frying pan or grill pan. Cook one at a time, over medium-low heat, about 2 minutes each side. Use two spatulas to carefully flip quesadillas.

Kid FRIENDLY

Prosciutto-wrapped
BEEF WITH PEA MASH

PREP & COOK TIME 30 MINUTES SERVES 4

4 slices prosciutto (60g)

4 x 200g (6½-ounce) beef eye fillet steaks

2 teaspoons olive oil

400g (12½ ounces) heirloom baby carrots, trimmed

20g (¾ ounce) butter

1 shallot (25g), chopped finely

1 clove garlic, crushed

1 tablespoon plain (all-purpose) flour

¼ cup (60ml) dry white wine

½ cup (125ml) chicken stock

1 cup (120g) frozen peas

¼ cup (60ml) pouring cream

1 tablespoon finely chopped fresh mint

¼ cup loosely packed small fresh mint leaves, extra

1 Wrap prosciutto around each beef steak, secure with toothpicks, if neccessary. Heat oil in a large frying pan over medium-high heat; cook beef, about 3 minutes each side or until cooked as desired. Remove from pan, cover; stand 10 minutes.

2 Meanwhile, boil, steam or microwave carrots until tender; drain.

3 Melt butter in same frying pan; cook onion and garlic, stirring, about 5 minutes or until onion softens. Add flour; cook, stirring, for 1 minute. Stir in wine; bring to the boil. Reduce heat; simmer, stirring, until mixture boils and thickens. Stir in stock and peas; bring to the boil. Reduce heat; simmer, uncovered, until mixture reduces by half. Stir in cream.

4 Coarsely mash pea mixture; stir in chopped mint. Season to taste. Discard toothpicks from beef before serving with minted pea mash and carrots. Sprinkle with extra mint.

Chorizo omelettes
WITH CHILLI BEANS

THE FRYING PAN GOES UNDER THE GRILL IN THIS RECIPE, SO YOU NEED A FRYING PAN WITH AN OVENPROOF HANDLE, OR COVER THE HANDLE WITH A FEW LAYERS OF FOIL TO PROTECT IT FROM THE HEAT OF THE GRILL.

Chorizo omelettes
WITH CHILLI BEANS

PREP & COOK TIME 15 MINUTES SERVES 4

420g (13½ ounces) canned chilli beans

1 tablespoon olive oil

1 cured chorizo sausage (170g), sliced thinly

125g (4 ounces) cherry tomatoes, halved

6 eggs

2 tablespoons milk

½ cup (60g) coarsely grated cheddar

1 large avocado (320g), chopped coarsely

2 tablespoons lime juice

¼ cup loosely packed fresh flat-leaf parsley leaves

1 Preheat grill (broiler).

2 Place undrained beans in a medium microwave-safe bowl; cover. Microwave on HIGH (100%) for 2 minutes, stirring halfway through cooking time.

3 Meanwhile, heat oil in a large ovenproof frying pan over medium-high heat; cook chorizo and tomatoes, stirring, until chorizo is browned and crisp.

4 Meanwhile, whisk eggs, milk and half the cheddar in a large bowl until combined; season. Pour egg mixture into pan, tilting to cover base of pan. Sprinkle with remaining cheddar. Cook, over low heat, about 5 minutes. Place pan under grill for 1 minute or until just set.

5 Using a fork mash avocado with juice in a small bowl; season to taste.

6 Cut omelette into wedges; top with chilli beans and avocado mash. Sprinkle with parsley; serve with lime wedges, if you like.

Pork sausages with
SAGE & ONION GRAVY

PREP & COOK TIME 30 MINUTES **SERVES** 4

2 large parsnips (700g), chopped coarsely

2 medium potatoes (400g), chopped coarsely

60g (2 ounces) butter

¼ cup (60ml) warm milk

2 tablespoons olive oil

8 thick pork sausages (960g)

200g (6½ ounces) rocket leaves (arugula)

sage and onion gravy

2 tablespoons olive oil

1 small clove garlic, crushed

½ cup (150g) caramelised onion

1 tablespoon plain (all-purpose) flour

1 cup (250ml) chicken stock

8 fresh sage leaves, torn

⅓ cup (80ml) apple cider

1 Boil, steam or microwave parsnip and potato until tender; drain. Mash parsnip and potato with butter and warm milk in a large bowl until smooth. Season to taste; cover to keep warm.

2 Heat oil in a large frying pan over medium heat; cook sausages, turning, about 10 minutes or until cooked through.

3 Meanwhile, make sage and onion gravy.

4 Drizzle sausages with sage and onion gravy; serve with parsnip mash and rocket.

sage and onion gravy Heat oil in a medium saucepan over medium-high heat; cook garlic and caramelised onion, 1 minute or until fragrant. Add flour; cook, stirring, 1 minute. Gradually add stock, then sage leaves and cider; simmer, uncovered, about 10 minutes or until gravy is thickened slightly. Season to taste.

tip Jars of caramelised onion can be found in the condiment aisle of supermarkets.

Kid
FRIENDLY

Quince, rosemary &
RED WINE GLAZED LAMB

PREP & COOK TIME 30 MINUTES SERVES 4

1 medium celeriac (celery root) (750g), trimmed, chopped coarsely

2 cups (500ml) chicken stock

2 teaspoons lemon juice

½ cup (125ml) pouring cream

2 lamb backstraps (400g)

1 tablespoon finely chopped fresh rosemary

1 tablespoon olive oil

100g (3 ounces) quince paste

1 clove garlic, crushed

1 cup (250ml) dry red wine

200g (6½ ounces) green beans, trimmed, halved lengthways

1 Combine celeriac and stock in a medium saucepan, add enough water to just cover celeriac. Bring to the boil, covered. Reduce heat; simmer, uncovered, about 15 minutes or until tender. Drain. Blend or process celeriac with juice and cream until smooth. Season to taste. Cover to keep warm.

2 Meanwhile, heat a large frying pan over medium-high heat. Combine lamb, rosemary and oil in a medium bowl; season. Cook lamb about 3 minutes each side or until cooked as desired. Remove from pan, cover; stand 5 minutes.

3 Add quince paste to same heated pan; cook, stirring, over medium heat, until softened. Add garlic and wine; cook, stirring, until mixture is combined. Simmer, uncovered, about 3 minutes or until the glaze has thickened; strain.

4 Meanwhile, microwave beans until just tender; drain.

5 Slice lamb; serve drizzled with glaze. Accompany with celeriac puree and beans, top with ground black pepper.

THE FRYING PANS GO UNDER THE GRILL IN THIS RECIPE, SO YOU NEED PANS WITH OVENPROOF HANDLES, OR COVER THE HANDLES WITH A FEW LAYERS OF FOIL TO PROTECT THEM FROM THE HEAT OF THE GRILL.

Rainbow chard &
THREE-CHEESE FRITTATA

PREP & COOK TIME 15 MINUTES SERVES 4

40g (1½ ounces) butter

375g (12 ounces) rainbow chard, trimmed, shredded coarsely

8 eggs

⅔ cup (50g) finely grated pecorino cheese

50g (1½ ounces) gorgonzola cheese, crumbled

50g (1½ ounces) firm ricotta

100g (3 ounces) rocket (arugula) leaves

1 tablespoon olive oil

1 tablespoon lemon juice

¼ cup (20g) grated pecorino cheese, extra

1 Preheat grill (broiler).

2 Heat half the butter in two 20cm/8-inch (base measurement) frying pans over high heat; cook rainbow chard, stirring, until wilted. Remove from pan; drain well.

3 Combine eggs, rainbow chard and pecorino in a large jug; season.

4 Melt remaining butter in same pans; pour in egg mixture, top with gorgonzola and ricotta. Cook over medium-low heat, about 5 minutes or until frittatas are almost set. Place frittatas under grill; grill about 5 minutes or until set and browned lightly.

5 Combine rocket, oil, juice and extra pecorino in a medium bowl; serve with frittatas.

tip We cooked the mixture in two smaller frying pans but you can make one large frittata in a large 25cm/10-inch (base measurement) frying pan; cook the frittata, over medium-low heat, about 10 minutes at step 4, then cook under the grill as recipe suggests.

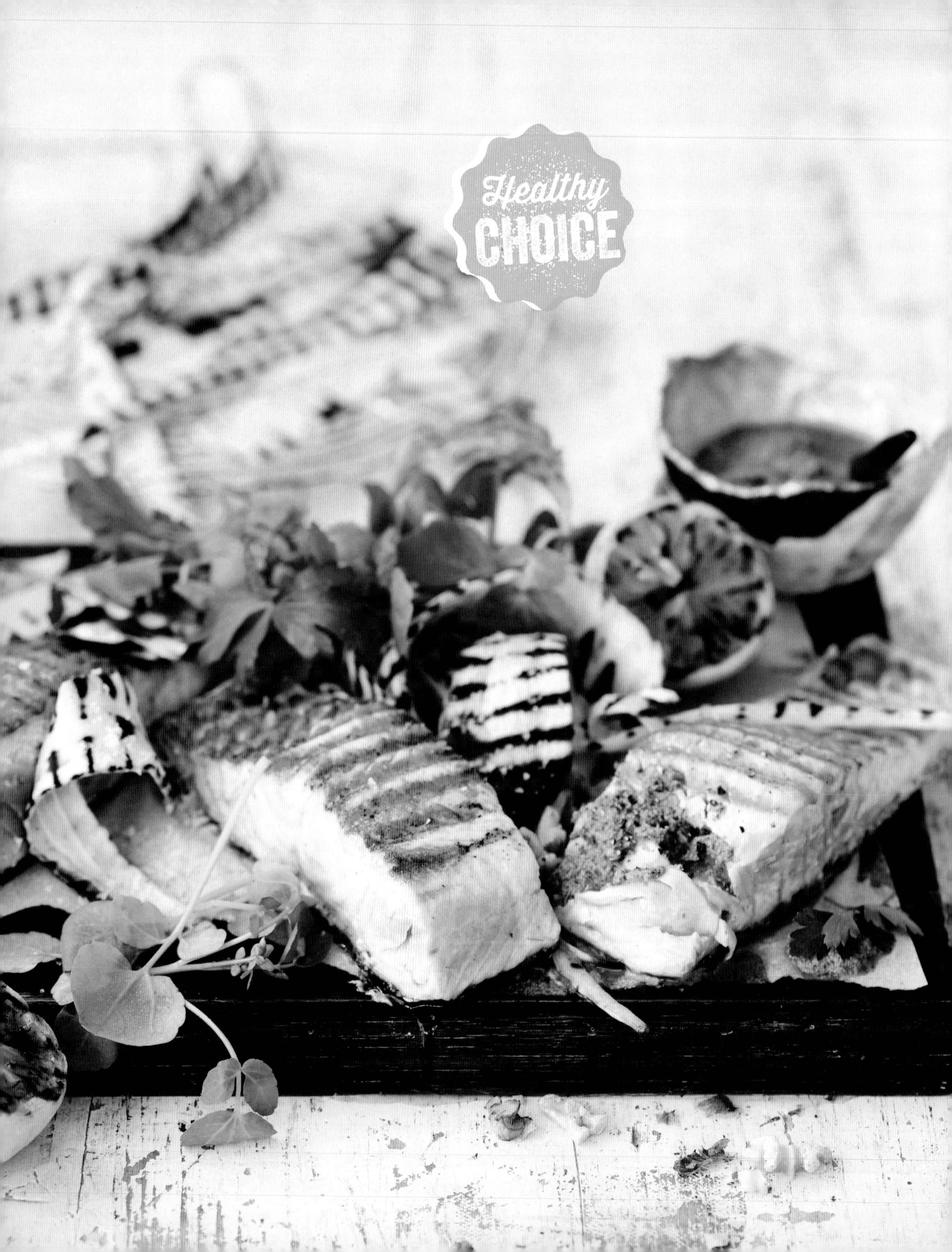
Healthy
CHOICE

Salmon with walnut pesto & PARSNIP CHIPS

PREP & COOK TIME 20 MINUTES SERVES 4

3 small parsnips (360g)

2 tablespoons olive oil

4 x 200g (6½-ounce) salmon fillets, skin on

1 lemon, halved crossways

2 cloves garlic, quartered

1 cup (100g) roasted walnuts

1½ cups firmly packed fresh mint leaves

1½ cups firmly packed fresh parsley leaves

¼ cup (60ml) lemon juice

½ cup (125ml) olive oil, extra

1 tablespoon torn fresh flat-leaf parsley leaves

2 cups firmly packed trimmed watercress

1 Heat a barbecue (or grill or grill plate) over medium-high heat.

2 Using a mandoline, V-slicer or sharp knife, thinly slice parsnips lengthways. Combine parsnip with half the oil in a large bowl, season. Cook parsnip on barbecue, in batches, about 2 minutes each side or until charred and tender.

3 Brush salmon with remaining oil; season. Cook salmon and lemon halves, cut-side down, on barbecue about 4 minutes each side or until salmon is cooked as desired and lemons are lightly charred.

4 Meanwhile, blend or process garlic, walnuts, herbs and juice until finely chopped. While motor is operating, add extra oil in a thin steady stream; blend until mixture is combined. Season.

5 Serve salmon topped with walnut pesto and torn parsley; accompany with parsnip chips, watercress and charred lemon halves.

Pork satay skewers
WITH COCONUT RICE

PREP & COOK TIME 30 MINUTES SERVES 4

800g (1½ pounds) pork fillets, cut into
2cm (¾-inch) pieces

300g (10 ounces) baby buk choy, trimmed, halved

450g (14½ ounces) packaged microwave
white long-grain rice

¼ cup (20g) toasted shredded coconut

2 green onions (scallions), sliced thinly

⅓ cup loosely packed coriander (cilantro) leaves

1 lime, cut into wedges

satay sauce

½ cup (75g) roasted peanuts, chopped coarsely

1 tablespoon light brown sugar

1 cup (250ml) coconut milk

1 teaspoon fish sauce

¼ cup (60ml) soy sauce

1 teaspoon chilli flakes

1 tablespoon peanut butter

1 Make satay sauce. Reserve 1 cup of the sauce.

2 Thread pork onto eight 23cm (9¼-inch) metal skewers, coat with remaining satay sauce.

3 Cook skewers on a heated oiled grill plate (or grill or barbecue), over medium-high heat, about 10 minutes or until cooked through.

4 Meanwhile, boil, steam or microwave buk choy until tender; drain.

5 Microwave rice according to directions on packet. Stir in coconut and onions; season to taste.

6 Serve skewers with buk choy and coconut rice, top with coriander and accompany with reserved satay sauce for dipping and lime wedges.

satay sauce Stir ingredients in a medium bowl until combined.

tip If using bamboo skewers, wrap the ends in foil to prevent them from burning.

Meat
FREE

Cardamom carrot, POTATO & SPINACH PILAF

PREP & COOK TIME 30 MINUTES SERVES 4

400g (12½ ounces) heirloom baby carrots, unpeeled, trimmed

400g (12½ ounces) baby new potatoes, quartered

2 tablespoons pure maple syrup

¼ cup (60ml) olive oil

2 medium brown onions (300g), sliced thinly

2 cloves garlic, crushed

½ teaspoon cumin seeds

6 cardamom pods, bruised

1½ cups (300g) basmati rice

3 cups (750ml) vegetable stock

100g (3 ounces) baby spinach leaves

cashew and coriander yoghurt

½ cup (140g) greek-style yoghurt

2 tablespoons coarsely chopped fresh coriander (cilantro)

2 tablespoons roasted cashews, chopped finely

1 Preheat oven to 220°C/425°F.

2 Place carrots and potatoes on a baking-paper-lined oven tray; drizzle with syrup and 2 tablespoons of the oil, season. Roast about 25 minutes or until tender.

3 Meanwhile, heat remaining oil in a large saucepan over medium heat; cook onion, garlic, cumin and cardamom, stirring, about 3 minutes or until onion is soft. Add rice; stir to coat in mixture. Add stock; bring to the boil. Reduce heat; simmer, covered, about 15 minutes or until rice is tender, adding spinach to pan for the last 5 minutes of cooking time. Season to taste.

4 Meanwhile, make cashew and coriander yoghurt.

5 Serve pilaf topped with carrots, potatoes and extra coriander leaves and cashews, if you like; accompany with cashew and coriander yoghurt.

cashew and coriander yoghurt Combine ingredients in a small bowl.

Thai spicy lamb
& NOODLE STIR-FRY

PREP & COOK TIME 30 MINUTES   SERVES 4

200g (6½ ounces) dried rice noodles

1 tablespoon peanut oil

500g (1 pound) lamb backstrap, sliced thinly

3 cloves garlic, crushed

2 fresh small red thai chillies, chopped finely

2 tablespoons fish sauce

2 tablespoons dark soy sauce

1 tablespoon light brown sugar

4 kaffir lime leaves, shredded

3 medium tomatoes (450g), chopped finely

⅓ cup loosely packed fresh thai basil leaves

¼ cup (35g) coarsely chopped roasted unsalted peanuts

1 Cook noodles according to directions on packet; drain.

2 Heat half the oil in a wok over high heat; stir-fry lamb, in batches, until browned. Remove from wok; cover to keep warm.

3 Heat remaining oil in wok; stir-fry garlic and chilli until fragrant. Add sauces, sugar and three quarters of the lime leaves; stir-fry until combined.

4 Return lamb to wok with noodles and tomato; stir-fry until tomato starts to soften and is heated through. Serve sprinkled with thai basil, nuts and remaining lime leaves.

Veal with mushroom sauce
& VEGETABLE CRISPS

PREP & COOK TIME 30 MINUTES SERVES 4

200g (6½ ounces) baby new potatoes

2 small kumara (orange sweet potatoes) (500g)

vegetable oil, for shallow-frying

2 tablespoons olive oil

8 x 250g (8-ounce) veal cutlets

200g (6½ ounces) thinly sliced swiss brown mushrooms

300ml pouring cream

60g (2 ounces) baby spinach leaves

1 Using a mandoline, V-slicer or sharp knife, cut potato and kumara into 2mm (⅛-inch) thick slices.

2 Heat enough vegetable oil in a large frying pan to come 2cm (¾-inch) up the side of the pan; shallow-fry potato and kumara, over medium heat, in batches, about 4 minutes or until golden and crisp. Drain on paper towel; season to taste.

3 Meanwhile, heat 1 tablespoon of the olive oil in a large frying pan over medium heat; cook veal about 5 minutes each side or until cooked as desired. Remove from pan; cover to keep warm.

4 Meanwhile, heat remaining olive oil in same pan; cook mushrooms over medium heat, stirring occasionally, about 4 minutes or until golden and tender. Add cream, bring to the boil; simmer 3 minutes or until thickened and reduced slightly. Add spinach leaves; stir until just wilted. Season to taste.

5 Serve cutlets with mushroom sauce, accompanied with vegetable crisps.

Barbecued pork hot dogs
WITH CRUNCHY SLAW

PREP & COOK TIME 20 MINUTES   MAKES 8

¼ cup (70g) tomato sauce (ketchup)

¼ cup (70g) barbecue sauce

2 tablespoons sweet chilli sauce

8 thick pork sausages (960g)

¼ small red cabbage (300g), shredded finely

¼ small green cabbage (300g), shredded finely

2 green onions (scallions), sliced thinly

1 small carrot (70g), cut into long thin matchsticks

¾ cup (225g) mayonnaise

2 tablespoons wholegrain mustard

1 tablespoon lemon juice

8 long bread rolls (400g)

flat-leaf parsley leaves, to serve

1 Combine sauces in a small bowl. Split sausages lengthways without cutting all the way through; open out flat. Brush sausages with half the sauce mixture. Cook sausages, cut-side down, on a heated oiled grill plate (or grill or barbecue) over medium-high heat for 3 minutes. Turn, brush with remaining sauce mixture; cook for a further 3 minutes or until cooked through. Transfer to a plate; cover to keep warm.

2 Meanwhile, combine cabbages, onion and carrot in a large bowl; season to taste.

3 Combine mayonnaise, mustard and juice in a small bowl.

4 Split rolls in half; toast until browned lightly.

5 Divide mayonnaise, sausages, slaw and parsley between rolls.

tip Use a mandoline or V-slicer to shred the cabbage and cut the carrot into matchsticks.

Cheap
EAT

One
PAN

Chicken with
MAPLE PARSNIPS

PREP & COOK TIME 35 MINUTES **SERVES** 4

1 tablespoon olive oil

4 x 200g (6½-ounce) chicken thigh cutlets, skin on

3 medium parsnips (750g), chopped coarsely

2 medium red onions (300g), cut into wedges

3 cloves garlic, sliced

4 sprigs fresh rosemary

2 tablespoons pure maple syrup

½ cup (125ml) salt-reduced chicken stock

½ cup (125ml) water

8 medium trimmed silver beet leaves (swiss chard) (280g)

1 Heat oil in a heavy-based saucepan over high heat; cook chicken for 2 minutes each side or until browned. Remove from pan; cover to keep warm.

2 Reduce heat to medium. Add parsnip, onion, garlic and rosemary to pan; cook for 5 minutes or until browned. Return chicken, skin-side up, to pan with maple syrup, stock and the water. Bring to the boil; cover, reduce heat to low. Simmer for 15 minutes or until chicken is just cooked through. Stir in silver beet; cook for 2 minutes or until wilted.

tip You could also use baby potatoes or carrots instead of the parsnips.

Creamy fennel, LEEK & CHICKEN PIES

PREP & COOK TIME 40 MINUTES SERVES 4

2 medium fennel bulbs (300g)

1 tablespoon olive oil

800g (1½ pounds) chicken breast fillets, chopped coarsely

20g (¾ ounce) butter

2 rindless bacon rashers (130g), sliced thinly

1 small leek (200g), trimmed, sliced thinly

1 tablespoon plain (all-purpose) flour

½ cup (125ml) dry white wine

300ml pouring cream

½ cup (125ml) milk

½ cup (60g) frozen peas

1 sheet puff pastry

1 egg, beaten lightly

60g (2 ounces) baby rocket (arugula) leaves

1 small radicchio (150g), leaves separated

2 tablespoons lemon juice

1 Preheat oven to 200°C/400°F. Grease four 1¼-cup (310ml) ovenproof dishes.

2 Using a mandoline or V-slicer, thinly slice fennel, reserve feathery fronds.

3 Heat oil in a large frying pan over medium heat; cook chicken, stirring, about 8 minutes or until cooked through. Remove from pan; cover to keep warm.

4 Melt butter in same heated pan; cook bacon, leek and half the fennel, stirring, about 5 minutes or until leek softens. Add flour; cook, stirring, until mixture thickens and bubbles. Gradually stir in wine, then cream and milk; cook, stirring, until mixture boils and thickens. Stir in chicken and peas. Season to taste. Divide chicken mixture among dishes.

5 Quarter pastry sheet; cut circles from each quarter slightly larger than the top of the dishes. Press pastry rounds over dishes, brush with egg. Cut a slit in each pastry top; bake about 20 minutes or until browned.

6 Meanwhile, combine remaining fennel with rocket, radicchio, juice and reserved fennel fronds in a medium bowl; season to taste. Serve pies with salad.

Healthy CHOICE

IF YOU'VE EVER BRUNCHED ON YUM CHA, YOU'VE PROBABLY EATEN GAI LAN – AND LOVED IT; STIR-FRIED OR STEAMED THEN SPLASHED WITH A LITTLE SESAME OIL AND OYSTER SAUCE, THIS DELICIOUSLY CRUNCHY VEGETABLE IS THE PERFECT ACCOMPANIMENT TO OUR CRISPY-SKINNED CHICKEN.

Crispy salt & pepper
CHICKEN WITH GAI LAN

PREP & COOK TIME 40 MINUTES SERVES 4

2 teaspoons sea salt

2 teaspoons cracked black peppercorns

1 teaspoon dried chilli flakes

4 x 200g (6½-ounce) chicken breast fillets, skin on

400g (12½ ounces) gai lan (chinese broccoli), trimmed, chopped coarsely

1 tablespoon oyster sauce

2 teaspoons sesame oil

1 medium carrot (120g), cut into matchsticks

½ cup (40g) bean sprouts

⅓ cup loosely packed fresh coriander (cilantro) leaves

2 green onions (scallions), sliced thinly

1 tablespoon lime juice

2 teaspoons toasted sesame seeds

1 lime, cut into wedges

1 Combine salt, pepper, chilli and chicken in a large bowl.

2 Cook chicken, in batches, skin-side down, in a heated oiled large frying pan, about 10 minutes or until browned and crisp. Turn chicken; cook about 5 minutes or until cooked through. Remove from pan; cover to keep warm.

3 Stir-fry gai lan, sauce and oil in same heated pan until gai lan is wilted.

4 Meanwhile, combine carrot, sprouts, coriander, onion and juice in a small bowl.

5 Serve chicken with gai lan, topped with carrot salad, sprinkled with sesame seeds. Accompany with lime wedges.

serving suggestion Serve with steamed jasmine rice.
tip To save time, you can use a julienne peeler, or a mandoline or V-slicer with a julienne attachment to cut the carrot into long thin matchsticks.

Spice-rubbed lamb
WITH CAULIFLOWER PUREE

PREP & COOK TIME 40 MINUTES   SERVES 4

1 teaspoon ground cumin

1 teaspoon fennel seeds

½ teaspoon sweet paprika

1 clove garlic, quartered

1 tablespoon olive oil

4 x 200g (6½-ounce) lamb backstraps

800g (1½ pounds) cauliflower, chopped coarsely

30g (1 ounces) butter

¼ cup (60ml) pouring cream

1 cup firmly packed watercress sprigs

chilli gremolata

⅓ cup finely chopped fresh flat-leaf parsley

⅓ cup finely chopped fresh mint

1 fresh long red chilli, chopped finely

1 clove garlic, crushed

2 teaspoons finely grated lemon rind

1 Dry-fry spices in a small frying pan over medium heat, stirring, for 1 minute or until fragrant. Using a mortar and pestle, grind spice mixture and garlic until crushed.
2 Heat a large frying pan over medium-high heat. Combine spice mixture, oil and lamb in a medium bowl; season. Cook lamb about 4 minutes each side or until cooked as desired. Remove from pan; cover, stand for 5 minutes.
3 Meanwhile, boil, steam or microwave cauliflower until tender; drain. Blend or process cauliflower with butter and cream until smooth. Season to taste. Cover to keep warm.
4 Make chilli gremolata.
5 Thickly slice lamb. Serve lamb with cauliflower mash and watercress; sprinkle with chilli gremolata.
chilli gremolata Combine ingredients in a small bowl.

Tandoori fish
WITH GREEN CHILLI RICE

PREP & COOK TIME 40 MINUTES SERVES 4

2 tablespoons tandoori paste

400ml can coconut milk

4 x 200g (6½-ounce) firm white fish fillets

2 teaspoons vegetable oil

1 large carrot (360g), cut into matchsticks

1 large green capsicum (bell pepper) (300g),
cut into matchsticks

1 medium red onion (170g), sliced thinly

½ cup (125ml) fish stock

150g (4½ ounces) sugar snap peas, trimmed,
halved on the diagonal

⅓ cup loosely packed fresh coriander (cilantro) leaves

green chilli rice

1 cup (200g) basmati rice

⅔ cup (160ml) water

1 fresh long green chilli, sliced thinly

1 teaspoon finely grated lime rind

1 Combine paste, ⅓ cup of the coconut milk and fish in
a large bowl; stand 5 minutes.

2 Meanwhile, make green chilli rice.

3 Heat oil in a large frying pan over medium-high heat;
cook carrot, capsicum and onion, stirring, about 3 minutes
or until softened. Add stock to pan; bring to the boil. Place
fish mixture on top of vegetables; cook, covered, 10 minutes.
Uncover, add peas to pan; cook about 5 minutes or until fish
is cooked through.

4 Serve fish with vegetable mixture, rice and coriander.

green chilli rice Rinse rice under cold water until water
runs clear; drain. Combine rice with the water, chilli, rind
and remaining coconut milk in a medium heavy-based
saucepan; bring to the boil, stirring occasionally. Reduce
heat; simmer, covered tightly, about 15 minutes or until
rice is tender. Remove from heat; stand, covered, 5 minutes.
Season to taste.

serving suggestions Serve with yoghurt and pappadums.
tip We used perch fillets for this recipe but you can use any
firm white fish fillets you like.

Pork with ginger beer & CARAMELISED APPLE

PREP & COOK TIME 35 MINUTES SERVES 4

700g (1½ pounds) potatoes, chopped coarsely

2 medium carrots (240g), chopped coarsely

50g (1½ ounces) butter

600g (1¼ pounds) pork fillets

2 medium apples (300g)

3 shallots (75g), sliced thinly

1 cup (250ml) ginger beer

2 tablespoons lime marmalade

2 tablespoons baby cress

1 Boil, steam or microwave potato and carrot, separately, until tender; drain. Mash potato and carrot in a large bowl with half the butter until combined; season to taste. Cover to keep warm.

2 Heat remaining butter in a large frying pan over medium-high heat; cook pork, turning, about 10 minutes or until cooked. Remove from pan; cover, stand for 5 minutes.

3 Meanwhile, thinly slice unpeeled apples crossways. Cook apple in same frying pan, over high heat, about 2 minutes each side or until caramelised. Remove from pan. Add shallot to pan; cook, stirring, over medium heat, about 3 minutes or until softened. Add ginger beer and marmalade. Bring to the boil. Reduce heat; simmer, uncovered, about 5 minutes or until thickened slightly.

4 Slice pork thickly. Serve pork with apple and mash; drizzle with sauce. Sprinkle with cress.

Chicken & thyme
RISOTTO

PREP & COOK TIME 45 MINUTES SERVES 4

2 x 200g (6½-ounce) chicken breast fillets

1 tablespoon teriyaki marinade

2 teaspoons finely grated orange rind

2 tablespoons olive oil

2 cloves garlic, crushed

1 medium brown onion (150g), chopped finely

1⅓ cups (260g) arborio rice

3 cups (750ml) chicken stock

150g (4½ ounces) baby spinach leaves

2 tablespoons coarsely chopped fresh lemon thyme, plus extra, to serve

1 Combine chicken with marinade and rind in a small bowl; toss chicken to coat.

2 Heat half the oil in a large saucepan over medium heat; cook garlic and onion, stirring, for 5 minutes or until onion softens. Add rice and stock, bring to the boil. Reduce heat; simmer, covered, for 15 minutes, stirring halfway through cooking. Remove from heat; cover.

3 Meanwhile, heat remaining oil in a large frying pan over medium heat; cook chicken about 5 minutes each side or until cooked through. Cover; rest for 5 minutes, then slice thinly.

4 Gently stir spinach and thyme into risotto. Serve risotto topped with chicken and extra thyme.

tips Substitute chicken with pork or firm white fish. This recipe is best made just before serving.

Chicken & sage meatballs
WITH CABBAGE AND PEAR

PREP & COOK TIME 40 MINUTES SERVES 4

400g (12½ ounces) minced (ground) chicken

⅔ cup (50g) fresh multigrain breadcrumbs

1 egg

2 teaspoons finely grated lemon rind

1 teaspoon allspice

1 medium brown onion (150g), grated coarsely

2 tablespoons finely chopped fresh sage

⅓ cup finely chopped fresh flat-leaf parsley

¼ cup (60ml) olive oil

1 medium leek (350g), halved, sliced thinly

2 medium pears (460g), sliced thinly

175g (5½ ounces) broccolini, trimmed

4 cups (320g) finely shredded red cabbage

1 teaspoon caraway seeds

2 tablespoons small sage leaves

2 tablespoons sultanas

1 Combine chicken, breadcrumbs, egg, rind, allspice, onion, chopped sage and parsley in a medium bowl, season; mix well. Roll mixture into 12 balls.

2 Heat half the oil in a large frying pan over medium heat; cook meatballs, turning, about 8 minutes or until browned and cooked through. Remove from pan; cover to keep warm.

3 Heat remaining oil in a large saucepan over medium-high heat; cook leek, stirring, for 3 minutes. Add pear and broccolini; cook, turning occasionally, for 3 minutes. Add cabbage, caraway, sage leaves and sultanas; cook, stirring, for 3 minutes or until just tender. Season to taste.

4 Serve vegetables with meatballs.

One PAN

Frying pan beef & SPINACH LASAGNE

PREP & COOK TIME 30 MINUTES SERVES 6

1 tablespoon olive oil

1 large brown onion (200g), chopped finely

2 cloves garlic, crushed

375g (12-ounce) packet fresh lasagne sheets

60g (2 ounces) baby spinach leaves

750g (1½ pounds) bottled bolognese pasta sauce

1 cup (250ml) water

1½ cups (360g) firm ricotta, crumbled

1½ cups (150g) coarsely grated pizza cheese

⅓ cup loosley packed fresh small basil leaves

1 Heat oil in a large deep frying pan over medium-high heat; cook onion and garlic, stirring, about 5 minutes or until onion softens.

2 Meanwhile, tear lasagne sheets lengthways into strips; put long strips aside, save any small broken pieces. Sprinkle small broken pasta pieces and spinach into pan with onion; mix gently to combine. Pour combined pasta sauce and the water into pan; mix gently to combine.

3 Insert long pasta strips, standing upright on long sides, into the mixture. Sprinkle with both cheeses. Bring the pan to the boil over high heat. Reduce heat to low; simmer, for 2 minutes or until pasta is tender.

4 Preheat grill (broiler).

5 Grill lasagne for 5 minutes or until cheese browns. Cover, stand for 5 minutes before serving. Sprinkle with basil.

tips You need a frying pan with an ovenproof handle for this recipe, or cover the handle with a few layers of foil to protect it from the heat of the grill. You could use a large flameproof baking dish (about 3-litres/12-cups) instead of the frying pan, if you prefer. Instead of breaking the pasta into long strips, simply break it all into bite-sized pieces; mix the pieces into the spinach and tomato sauce mixture, sprinkle over the cheese and cook the lasagne as directed.

Barbecued squid with
CRACKED WHEAT RISOTTO

PREP & COOK TIME 50 MINUTES SERVES 4

250g (8 ounces) sugar snap peas

500g (1 pound) squid

2 cloves garlic, crushed

1 tablespoon finely chopped fresh oregano

2 teaspoons coarsely grated lemon rind

2 tablespoons olive oil

1 medium brown onion (150g), chopped finely

3 cloves garlic, crushed, extra

1 tablespoon fresh lemon thyme leaves

1 cup (160g) coarse cracked wheat

1 litre (4 cups) water

2 tablespoons lemon juice

1 tablespoon fresh oregano leaves, extra

1 Blanch peas in boiling water for 30 seconds; drain. Refresh under cold water; drain. Cut in half lengthways.

2 Clean squid hoods, reserve the tenticles. Cut hoods in half lengthways. Using a sharp knife, score inside surface in criss-cross pattern at 1cm (½-inch) intervals. Cut into 4cm (1½-inch) strips. Combine squid hood and tenticles in a medium bowl with garlic, chopped oregano, rind and 1 tablespoon of oil.

3 Heat remaining oil in a large frying pan over medium heat; cook onion, extra garlic and thyme, stirring, for 5 minutes or until onion softens.

4 Add cracked wheat and the water; cook, stirring occasionally, for 15 minutes or until cracked wheat is tender. Add peas and juice, stir for 2 minutes or until heated through. Season to taste.

5 Meanwhile, cook squid on a heated grill plate (or grill or barbecue), over medium-high heat, for 2 minutes, turning halfway through cooking time, or until just cooked through.

6 Serve cracked wheat mixture with squid; sprinkle with extra oregano.

tips You could also try this with thin strips of chicken or pork. Cracked wheat can be bought from health food stores.

FAST BURGERS

Moroccan BEEF BURGER

PREP & COOK TIME 30 MINUTES
MAKES 4

Cook 4 beef hamburger patties (500g) in a heated oiled large frying pan, over medium heat, about 5 minutes each side or until cooked through. Combine ½ cup (140g) natural yoghurt with 2 teaspoons finely chopped preserved lemon rind, 1 tablespoon moroccan spice mix and 1 teaspoon harissa paste in a small bowl. Halve and toast 4 bread rolls. Sandwich rolls with yoghurt mixture, patties, baby spinach leaves, drained char-grilled capsicum (bell pepper) and strips of lemon rind.

BBQ bacon CHEESEBURGER

PREP & COOK TIME 30 MINUTES
MAKES 4

Preheat grill (broiler). Place 8 slices thin streaky bacon on an oven tray. Brush with 2 teaspoons pure maple syrup; cook under grill about 2 minutes or until crisp. Drain on paper towel. Cook 4 beef hamburger patties (500g) in a heated oiled large frying pan, over medium heat, about 5 minutes each side or until cooked through. Halve and toast 4 bread rolls. Sandwich rolls with patties, bacon, a slice of swiss cheese, store-bought coleslaw, parsley leaves and a drizzle of barbecue sauce.

Beef teriyaki burger WITH PINEAPPLE

PREP & COOK TIME 30 MINUTES
MAKES 4

Cook 4 beef hamburger patties (500g) in a heated oiled large frying pan, over medium heat, basting with 1 tablespoon of thick teriyaki marinade, about 5 minutes each side, or until cooked through. Cook 4 drained canned pineapple slices in same pan about 1 minute each side or until caramelised. Halve and toast 4 bread rolls. Sandwich rolls with some baby tat soi, patties, pineapple, cucumber ribbons, coriander (cilantro) leaves, thinly sliced green onions, finely chopped red chilli and a drizzle of thick teriyaki marinade.

Minty beef & BEETROOT BURGER

PREP & COOK TIME 30 MINUTES
MAKES 4

Cut 1 peeled medium beetroot (beet) into matchsticks. Combine beetroot and 2 teaspoons lemon juice in a small bowl. Season to taste. Cook 4 beef hamburger patties (500g) in a heated oiled large frying pan, over medium heat, about 5 minutes each side or until cooked through. Halve and toast 4 bread rolls. Spread each bread roll base with 2 teaspoons thick mint sauce. Sandwich rolls with small baby cos (romaine) lettuce leaves, patties, sliced tomato, carrot matchsticks, beetroot mixture, 80g (2½oz) crumbled soft goat's cheese and small fresh mint leaves.

EXPRESS
DESSERTS

Pear, maple & CASHEW TARTS

PREP & COOK TIME 30 MINUTES SERVES 4

1 large pear (330g)

1 sheet puff pastry

20g (¾ ounce) butter, melted

¼ cup (60ml) pure maple syrup

¼ cup (40g) cashews, halved

2 teaspoons cinnamon sugar

1 cup (280g) labne

1 Preheat oven to 220°C/425°F. Grease a large oven tray; line with baking paper.

2 Using a mandoline or V-slicer, slice unpeeled pear thinly lengthways.

3 Cut pastry sheet in half lengthways; place on tray. Arrange pear on pastry. Brush with butter and half the syrup. Top with nuts and sprinkle with half the sugar.

4 Bake tarts about 20 minutes or until pastry is browned.

5 Combine labne and remaining sugar in a small bowl. Drizzle hot tarts with remaining syrup; serve with labne.

tip Cinnamon sugar is available in the spice section of the supermarket.

Warm choc-caramel
PUDDINGS

PREP & COOK TIME 30 MINUTES MAKES 4

125g (4 ounces) butter, softened

⅔ cup (150g) firmly packed brown sugar

2 eggs

½ cup (75g) plain (all-purpose) flour

¼ cup (25g) cocoa powder

1½ tablespoons milk

12 caramel-filled chocolate balls

2 teaspoons icing (confectioners') sugar

1 Preheat oven to 200°C/400°F.

2 Grease four 1-cup (250ml) ovenproof dishes; line bases with baking paper.

3 Beat butter and brown sugar in a small bowl with an electric mixer until light and fluffy. Beat in eggs, one at a time. Stir in sifted flour, cocoa and milk.

4 Divide two-thirds of the mixture into dishes; place three caramel-filled chocolate balls in centre of each dish. Spoon remaining mixture over chocolate balls; smooth surface.

5 Bake about 20 minutes. Stand puddings for 5 minutes before serving dusted with sifted icing sugar.

serving suggestion Serve with thick (double) cream or ice-cream, dusted with sifted cocoa powder.

tips The melted chocolate will be hot, so take care. These cakes should be served straight away; if they are allowed to sit too long, the gooey centre will firm up and the chocolate won't ooze out when they're cut into. You can use any-flavoured chocolate balls or filled chocolate squares you like – if using small filled chocolate squares, use 4 per pudding.

Warm rhubarb, ginger & COCONUT TRIFLES

PREP & COOK TIME 25 MINUTES   SERVES 4

3¼ cups (400g) coarsely chopped rhubarb

2 tablespoons orange juice

¼ cup (55g) caster (superfine) sugar

2 cups (500ml) thick vanilla custard

250g (4 ounces) ginger cake, chopped coarsely

⅓ cup (15g) toasted flaked coconut

2 tablespoons coarsely chopped pistachios

1 Combine rhubarb, juice and sugar in a medium saucepan; bring to the boil. Reduce heat; simmer, uncovered, stirring occasionally, about 3 minutes or until rhubarb is tender.
2 Meanwhile, heat custard in a small saucepan over low heat.
3 Divide ginger cake between four heatproof serving glasses; top with warm custard, then rhubarb mixture, coconut and nuts. Serve immediately.

tips You need about 5 trimmed stems of rhubarb for this recipe. We used a bought ginger loaf cake for this recipe; available in the bakery section of most large supermarkets. If you can't find it you could use broken gingerbread biscuits instead.

Raspberry pancakes
WITH COCONUT YOGHURT

PREP & COOK TIME 30 MINUTES SERVES 4

2 cups (300g) frozen raspberries

2 tablespoons icing (confectioners') sugar

2 teaspoons finely grated lime rind

2 tablespoons lime juice

1 cup (150g) self-raising flour

¼ cup (55g) caster (superfine) sugar

2 eggs

1 cup (250ml) buttermilk

1 cup (280g) coconut yoghurt

1 Combine half the berries, icing sugar, rind and juice in a small bowl over medium heat. Cook, stirring for 5 minutes or until heated through.

2 Sift flour and caster sugar into a medium bowl; gradually whisk in combined eggs and buttermilk until smooth. Add remaining berries to batter; stir until combined.

3 Heat a greased small frying pan over medium heat. Pour in ¼ cup batter; cook pancake about 2 minutes each side or until browned. Repeat with remaining batter to make 12 pancakes in total.

4 Serve pancakes drizzled with raspberry mixture, accompanied with yoghurt.

Apple, cherry & AMARETTI CRUMBLES

PREP & COOK TIME 35 MINUTES   SERVES 4

5 medium apples (750g), peeled, cored, sliced thickly

¼ cup (55g) caster (superfine) sugar

2 tablespoons water

½ teaspoon mixed spice

1½ cups (225g) frozen seedless cherries

125g (4 ounces) amaretti biscuits, crushed

¼ cup (30g) ground almonds

¼ cup (35g) slivered almonds

¼ cup (35g) plain (all-purpose) flour

80g (2½ ounces) cold butter, chopped finely

1 Preheat oven to 200°C/400°F. Grease four 1¼-cup (310ml) ovenproof dishes.

2 Combine apple, sugar, the water and spice in a medium saucepan; cook, covered, over medium heat, about 5 minutes or until apple is just tender. Remove from heat; stir in cherries. Divide mixture among dishes.

3 Meanwhile, combine crushed biscuits, ground almonds, slivered almonds and flour in a medium bowl; rub in butter. Sprinkle mixture evenly over apple mixture.

4 Place dishes on an oven tray; bake about 20 minutes or until browned. Serve with ice-cream, if you like.

tip You can use any frozen berry you like, instead of the cherries.

Kid
FRIENDLY

Peanut butter & jelly
FRENCH TOAST

PREP & COOK TIME 30 MINUTES SERVES 4

8 slices white bread (360g)

⅔ cup (140g) crunchy peanut butter

⅓ cup (110g) strawberry jam

2 eggs

⅓ cup (80ml) milk

40g (1½ ounces) butter

1 Spread 4 slices of the bread with peanut butter. Spread remaining slices of bread with jam. Sandwich one peanut butter and one jam slice of bread together, to make 4 peanut butter and jam sandwiches.

2 Lightly whisk eggs and milk in a medium bowl to combine. Dip sandwiches, one at a time, into egg mixture. Melt 10g (½ ounce) butter in a large frying pan over medium-high heat; cook one sandwich, about 3 minutes each side or until golden and crisp. Transfer to a plate; cover to keep warm. Repeat with remaining sandwiches, using 10g (½ ounce) butter for each.

3 Cut toasts in half; serve hot, with whipped cream and fresh strawberries and dusted with sifted icing (confectioners') sugar, if you like.

Churros with
CHILLI CHOCOLATE

PREP & COOK TIME 40 MINUTES **SERVES** 6

100g (3 ounces) butter, chopped

1 cup (250ml) water

1 cup (150g) plain (all-purpose) flour

3 eggs

vegetable oil, for deep-frying

⅓ cup (75g) caster (superfine) sugar

1 teaspoon ground cinnamon

chilli chocolate

300g (9½ ounces) dark eating (semi-sweet) chocolate

30g (1 ounce) butter

¾ cup (180ml) pouring cream

pinch mexican chilli powder (optional)

1 Bring butter and the water to the boil in a medium saucepan. Add sifted flour; beat with a wooden spoon over heat until mixture comes away from base and side of the pan and forms a smooth ball.

2 Transfer mixture to a small bowl; beat in eggs, one at a time, on medium speed with an electric mixer for about 1 minute or until mixture becomes glossy.

3 Make chilli chocolate.

4 Heat oil in a large wide saucepan. Spoon mixture into a piping bag fitted with a 1cm (½-inch) fluted tube. Squeeze 15cm (6-inch) lengths of dough into the hot oil; cut off with a sharp knife or scissors. Deep-fry about four strips at a time, about 2 minutes each side or until browned lightly and cooked through. Drain churros on paper towel. Toss hot churros in combined sugar and cinnamon.

5 Serve churros immediately with small bowls or large cups of chilli chocolate for dipping.

chilli chocolate Break chocolate into a medium heatproof bowl, add butter, cream and chilli; stir over a medium saucepan of simmering water (do not allow water to touch base of bowl) until smooth.

Pear & coconut
SPONGE PUDDINGS

PREP & COOK TIME 35 MINUTES SERVES 4

5 medium pears (1.2kg)

¼ cup (55g) caster (superfine) sugar

¼ cup (60ml) water

1 cinnamon stick

2 eggs

1 teaspoon vanilla extract

1 tablespoon finely grated lemon rind

¼ cup (55g) caster (superfine) sugar, extra

½ cup (75g) self-raising flour

⅓ cup (25g) shredded coconut

2 teaspoons icing (confectioners') sugar

⅔ cup (190g) coconut yoghurt

1 Preheat oven to 180°C/350°F. Grease four 1-cup (250ml) ovenproof dishes.

2 Peel, core and quarter 4 of the pears. Combine pears, caster sugar, the water and cinnamon in a medium saucepan; cook, covered, over medium heat, for 5 minutes or until pears are tender. Discard cinnamon. Spoon pear into dishes.

3 Beat eggs, extract, rind and extra caster sugar in a small bowl with an electric mixer until thick and creamy. Transfer to a medium bowl; fold in sifted flour and coconut. Spoon sponge mixture over pear. Place dishes on oven tray.

4 Bake puddings about 15 minutes or until browned lightly.

5 Meanwhile, core and thinly slice remaining pear.

6 Stand puddings for 5 minutes before serving dusted with sifted icing sugar; accompany with sliced pear and coconut yoghurt.

Mixed berry CLAFOUTIS

PREP & COOK TIME 45 MINUTES SERVES 4

⅔ cup (160ml) milk

⅔ cup (160ml) pouring cream

1 cinnamon stick

1 teaspoon vanilla extract

4 eggs

½ cup (110g) caster (superfine) sugar

¼ cup (35g) plain (all-purpose) flour

2 cups (300g) frozen mixed berries

1 Preheat oven to 200°C/400°F. Grease a 1.5-litre (6-cup) ovenproof dish.

2 Combine milk, cream, cinnamon and extract in a medium saucepan; bring to the boil. Remove from heat; discard cinnamon.

3 Whisk eggs and sugar in a medium bowl until light and frothy; whisk in flour, then gradually whisk in cream mixture.

4 Sprinkle berries into dish; pour cream mixture over berries. Bake about 35 minutes or until browned lightly and set. Serve clafoutis warm dusted with sifted icing (confectioners') sugar, with whipped cream or ice-cream, if you like.

Cheap
EAT

Healthy CHOICE

Warm lemon & blueberry
MERINGUE POTS

PREP & COOK TIME 40 MINUTES SERVES 4

2 cups (300g) frozen blueberries

2 tablespoons caster (superfine) sugar

1 teaspoon cornflour (cornstarch)

2 teaspoons finely grated lemon rind

1 tablespoon lemon juice

3 egg whites

¾ cup (165g) caster (superfine) sugar, extra

2 teaspoons cornflour (cornstarch), extra

2 teaspoons white vinegar

1 Preheat oven to 160°C/325°F.

2 Combine berries and sugar in a small saucepan; stir over low heat until sugar dissolves. Stir in blended cornflour, rind and juice; cook, stirring, until mixture boils and thickens slightly. Mash mixture coarsely with a fork. Divide among four 1-cup (250ml) ovenproof dishes.

3 Beat egg whites in a small bowl with an electric mixer until soft peaks form. Gradually add extra sugar, beating until sugar dissolves between additions; fold in remaining ingredients.

4 Spoon meringue over berry mixture in dishes; bake about 30 minutes or until meringue is browned lightly.

tip The meringue will sink a little after standing.

Mandarin & chai
SOUFFLÉS

PREP & COOK TIME 40 MINUTES (& REFRIGERATION) **SERVES** 6

60g (2 ounces) butter, melted

⅔ cup (150g) caster (superfine) sugar

2 tablespoons water

2 teaspoons cornflour (cornstarch)

1 teaspoon ground cinnamon

1 teaspoon ground ginger

½ teaspoon ground cardamom

½ teaspoon ground clove

⅓ cup (80ml) strained mandarin juice

4 egg whites

2 tablespoons caster (superfine) sugar, extra

2 tablespoons icing (confectioners') sugar

caramelised mandarins

4 medium mandarins (800g)

1 cup (220g) caster (superfine) sugar

1 cup (250ml) strained mandarin juice

1 cinnamon stick

1 Make caramelised mandarins.

2 Preheat oven to 200°C/400°F. Grease six ¾-cup (180ml) ovenproof soufflé dishes with the melted butter; sprinkle with 2 tablespoons of the caster sugar, shake out excess sugar. Place dishes on oven tray.

3 Combine the remaining caster sugar and the water in a small saucepan; stir over high heat, without boiling, until sugar dissolves. Bring to the boil. Reduce heat; simmer, uncovered, without stirring, for 2 minutes.

4 Blend cornflour with the spices and juice in a small bowl, add to sugar syrup; cook, stirring, over high heat, until mixture boils and thickens. Boil for 1 minute, stirring.

5 Beat egg whites and extra caster sugar in a small bowl with an electric mixer until soft peaks form; transfer to a large bowl. Fold warm sugar syrup mixture into egg white mixture.

6 Spoon mixture evenly into dishes; smooth surface. Bake soufflés about 15 minutes. Dust with sifted icing sugar; serve soufflés immediately with caramelised mandarins.

caramelised mandarins Peel and segment mandarins. Place sugar and ¼ cup (60ml) of the juice in a large frying pan; cook, stirring, over medium heat, without boiling, until sugar dissolves. Add cinnamon, bring to the boil. Boil, without stirring, until it turns a dark caramel colour (tilt the pan during cooking). Remove from heat; carefully stir in remaining juice (take care as caramel will splatter); stir over heat until toffee pieces are dissolved. Stir in mandarin segments. Discard cinnamon stick before serving.

Kid FRIENDLY

Warm chocolate
BANOFFEE PAVLOVAS

PREP & COOK TIME 40 MINUTES   SERVES 4

2 egg whites

1⅓ cups (215g) icing (confectioners') sugar

⅓ cup (80ml) boiling water

1 tablespoon cocoa powder, sifted

1 cup (250ml) salted caramel dessert sauce

2 medium bananas (400g), sliced thinly

300ml double (thick) cream

50g (1½-ounce) chocolate-coated honeycomb bar, chopped coarsely

1 Preheat oven to 180°C/350°F. Line a large oven tray with baking paper.

2 Beat egg whites, icing sugar and the water in a small bowl with an electric mixer about 10 minutes or until firm peaks form.

3 Fold sifted cocoa into meringue. Drop four equal amounts of mixture onto tray; use the back of a spoon to create a well in the centre of the mounds. Bake 25 minutes or until firm to touch.

4 Meanwhile, heat caramel sauce according to directions on packet.

5 Serve pavlovas straight from the oven, topped with warm sauce, banana, cream and chocolate-coated honeycomb.

Sticky date & ginger SELF-SAUCING PUDDINGS

PREP & COOK TIME 40 MINUTES SERVES 6

1½ cups (225g) self-raising flour

¾ cup (165g) firmly packed brown sugar

30g (1 ounce) butter, melted

¾ cup (180ml) milk

¾ cup (100g) finely chopped dried seedless dates

¼ cup (45g) finely chopped glacé ginger

caramel sauce

¾ cup (165g) firmly packed brown sugar

1 teaspoon ground ginger

2⅔ cups (660ml) boiling water

75g (2½ ounces) butter

1 Preheat oven to 180°C/350°F. Grease six 1½-cup (375ml) individual ovenproof dishes.

2 Combine flour, sugar, butter, milk, dates and ginger in a medium bowl. Spread mixture into dishes.

3 Make caramel sauce.

4 Pour caramel sauce slowly over the back of a spoon onto mixture in dishes. Bake about 25 minutes or until centres of puddings are firm. Stand 5 minutes before serving.

caramel sauce Combine ingredients in a medium heatproof jug; stir until sugar is dissolved.

Mini pecan, macadamia
& WALNUT PIES

PREP & COOK TIME 50 MINUTES (& REFRIGERATION) **MAKES** 6

3 sheets shortcrust pastry, thawed

⅓ cup (50g) unsalted macadamias

⅓ cup (45g) pecans

⅓ cup (35g) walnuts

2 tablespoons light brown sugar

1 tablespoon plain (all-purpose) flour

40g (1½ ounces) butter, melted

2 eggs, beaten lightly

¾ cup (180ml) maple syrup

1 Grease six 10cm (4-inch) round loose-based fluted flan tins.

2 Cut each pastry sheet in half diagonally. Lift pastry into tins. Press into base and sides; trim edges. Cover; refrigerate 30 minutes.

3 Meanwhile, preheat oven to 200°C/400°F.

4 Place tins on an oven tray. Line each tin with baking paper; fill with dried beans or rice. Bake 10 minutes. Remove paper and beans. Bake about 7 minutes or until browned lightly.

5 Meanwhile, combine remaining ingredients in a bowl.

6 Reduce oven temperature to 180°C/350°F.

7 Divide filling among cases. Bake pies about 20 minutes or until set; cool.

tips Do not use maple-flavoured syrup as a substitute for real maple syrup in the nut filling. Pies can be served warm with ice-cream or at room temperature.

Marmalade & apple
PULL-APART

PREP & COOK TIME 50 MINUTES MAKES 12

2 cups (300g) self-raising flour

1 tablespoon caster (superfine) sugar

30g (1 ounce) butter, chopped

1 cup (250ml) milk, approximately

¼ cup (80g) orange marmalade

400g (12½ ounces) canned pie apples

pinch ground nutmeg

½ teaspoon ground cinnamon

2 tablespoons finely chopped roasted pecans

1 tablespoon icing (confectioners') sugar

¼ cup (30g) coarsely chopped roasted pecans, extra

¼ cup (80g) orange marmalade, warmed, extra

1 Preheat oven to 200°C/400°F. Grease a deep 22cm (9-inch) round cake pan.

2 Sift flour into a medium bowl, stir in caster sugar; rub in butter with your fingertips. Make a well in centre of flour mixture; stir in enough milk to mix to a soft, sticky dough. Knead dough on a floured surface until smooth.

3 Roll dough on floured baking paper into a 21cm x 40cm (8-inch x 16-inch) rectangle. Spread marmalade over dough; spread with combined apples, spices and nuts leaving a 3cm (1¼-inch) border around long edge. Using paper as a guide, roll dough up from long side like a swiss roll. Use a floured serrated knife to cut the roll into 12 slices. Place 11 slices upright around edge of pan; place remaining slice in centre.

4 Bake about 25 minutes or until golden brown in colour. Leave in pan for 5 minutes before turning, top-side up, onto a serving plate. Serve pull-apart warm, dusted with sifted icing sugar, sprinkled with extra nuts and drizzled with extra marmalade.

Black forest
SOUFFLÉS

Black forest
SOUFFLÉS

PREP & COOK TIME 55 MINUTES **SERVES** 4

60g (2 ounces) butter, melted

2 tablespoons caster (superfine) sugar

300g (9½ ounces) dark (semi-sweet) chocolate

6 eggs, at room temperature, separated

3 egg whites, at room temperature

⅓ cup (75g) caster (superfine) sugar, extra

2 teaspoons icing (confectioners') sugar

poached cherries

415g (13 ounces) canned seedless black cherries in syrup

¼ cup (55g) caster (superfine) sugar

5cm (2-inch) strip orange rind

2 tablespoons kirsch or cherry brandy

1 Make poached cherries.

2 Preheat oven to 200°C/400°F. Grease four 1¼-cup (310ml) ovenproof soufflé dishes with butter, sprinkle butter with caster sugar; shake out excess sugar.

3 Break chocolate into a large heatproof bowl over a large saucepan of simmering water (don't let water touch base of bowl); stir until chocolate is melted. Cool 5 minutes; stir in egg yolks.

4 Beat all 9 egg whites and extra sugar in a medium bowl with an electric mixer until soft peaks form. Fold into chocolate mixture, in two batches. Divide mixture between dishes; smooth tops. Place dishes on an oven tray. Bake soufflés about 15 minutes.

5 Dust soufflés with sifted icing sugar. Serve immediately with poached cherries.

poached cherries Drain cherries; reserve syrup and cherries separately. Stir syrup, sugar and rind in a medium saucepan; stir over high heat, without boiling, until sugar dissolves. Bring to the boil. Reduce heat; simmer, uncovered, about 5 minutes or until syrup thickens slightly. Remove from heat; stir in cherries and kirsch.

serving suggestion Serve with vanilla ice-cream or thick (double) cream.

Apricot & almond
FILLO TARTE TATIN

PREP & COOK TIME 50 MINUTES **SERVES** 4

10g (½ ounce) butter

2 tablespoons water

⅓ cup (75g) firmly packed brown sugar

1 vanilla bean, split lengthways, seeds scraped

4 sheets fillo pastry

825g (1¾ pounds) canned apricot halves in natural juice, drained

2 tablespoons flaked almonds

cooking-oil spray

1 Preheat oven to 200°C/400°F.

2 Combine butter, the water, sugar and vanilla bean pod and seeds in a medium ovenproof frying pan (base measurement 25cm/10 inches) over medium heat; cook, stirring, for 1 minute or until butter has melted and sugar has dissolved.

3 Increase heat to high; cook, stirring occasionally, for 2 minutes or until liquid has thickened slightly.

4 Meanwhile, place one pastry sheet on bench; spray with oil. Top with another pastry sheet, in a cross pattern; spray with oil. Top with another pastry sheet, diagonally; spray with oil. Top with remaining pastry sheet, in opposite diagonal direction; spray with oil.

5 Add apricots and nuts to pan with sauce, covering base of pan. Place pastry sprayed-side up, over apricots and carefully tuck pastry in around the edges.

6 Bake for 20 minutes or until pastry is golden and crisp. Carefully turn onto a plate. Cut into wedges to serve. Discard vanilla bean before serving.

serving suggestion Serve with ice-cream or thick greek-style yoghurt.

Rhubarb & vanilla
BAKED CUSTARD

PREP & COOK TIME 50 MINUTES **SERVES** 4

8 stems trimmed rhubarb (500g), chopped coarsely

⅓ cup (75g) caster (superfine) sugar

1 vanilla bean, split lengthways

4 eggs

2 cups (500ml) hot milk

pinch ground nutmeg

1 Preheat oven to 220°C/425°F. Grease and line a large baking tray. Grease four 1½-cup (375ml) ovenproof dishes.
2 Toss rhubarb with 1 tablespoon of the sugar on a baking tray. Roast for 15 minutes or until rhubarb is tender. Divide rhubarb between ovenproof dishes; reserve any juices on tray. Reduce oven temperature to 160°C/325°F.
3 Scrape seeds from vanilla bean. Whisk eggs, vanilla seeds and remaining sugar in a medium bowl; whisk in hot milk. Gently pour custard mixture over rhubarb in dishes; sprinkle with nutmeg.
4 Place dishes in a medium baking dish; add enough boiling water to come halfway up side of dishes. Bake for 30 minutes or until custard is just set. Serve drizzled with reserved juices.

tips The rhubarb can be made up to 3 days in advance; store, covered, in the fridge. Place the empty vanilla pod in a jar then cover it with caster sugar to make your own vanilla sugar.

Warm choc-nut brownie
WITH COFFEE ANGLAISE

PREP & COOK TIME 1 HOUR SERVES 8

275g (9 ounces) dark (semi-sweet) chocolate, chopped finely

150g (4½ ounces) butter, chopped

⅔ cup (150g) caster (superfine) sugar

2 eggs, beaten lightly

1 cup (150g) plain (all-purpose) flour

½ cup (75g) self-raising flour

⅔ cup (90g) unsalted macadamias, lightly roasted, chopped coarsely

100g (3 ounces) milk chocolate, chopped coarsely

100g (3 ounces) dark (semi-sweet) chocolate, extra, chopped coarsely

coffee anglaise

2 cups (500ml) pouring cream

1 tablespoon instant coffee granules

4 egg yolks

¼ cup (55g) caster (superfine) sugar

1 Preheat oven to 170°C/340°F. Grease a shallow 20cm (8-inch) square cake pan; line base with baking paper.
2 Stir chocolate and butter in a medium saucepan over low heat until smooth. Remove from heat.
3 Stir sugar, then egg into chocolate mixture. Fold in combined sifted flours, then nuts and remaining chocolate. Spread mixture into pan.
4 Bake for 35 minutes or until a skewer inserted into the centre comes out with moist crumbs. Stand in pan 10 minutes.
5 Meanwhile, make coffee anglaise.
6 Serve warm brownie with anglaise.

coffee anglaise Bring cream to the boil in a medium saucepan. Remove from heat; stir in coffee until dissolved. Whisk egg yolks and sugar in a medium bowl until creamy. Gradually whisk in warm cream mixture. Return mixture to pan; stir over medium-high heat, without boiling, until custard thickens and coats the back of a spoon. Strain mixture into a medium jug.

tips These brownies will only be as good as the chocolate used. The more cocoa solids in the chocolate, the more intense the chocolate taste will be. Aim for a dark chocolate containing between 50-70% cocoa solids. Chocolate with a lower cocoa solid percentage means that more sugar and fat has been added. Brownies can be made 3 days ahead; store them in an airtight container. Reheat for 30 seconds in the microwave.

FAST TREATS

Choc-hazelnut
INDULGENCE CAKE
PREP TIME 25 MINUTES
SERVES 12

Split two 600g (1¼lb) round dark chocolate mud cakes in half (you will have four cake rounds). Whisk 2 cups (500ml) thick vanilla custard and 200g (6½oz) chocolate-hazelnut spread in a medium bowl until combined. Layer sponge rounds with custard mixture on a serving plate. Serve topped with 100g (3oz) coarsely chopped hazelnut milk chocolate and ½ cup (70g) coarsely chopped roasted hazelnuts.

tip Remove icing from cakes before splitting into layers.

Baked pears with
PECAN QUINOA
PREP & COOK TIME 30 MINUTES
SERVES 4

Preheat oven to 180°C/350°F. Drain 825g (1¾lb) canned pear halves. Place ⅓ cup (20g) quinoa flakes, 2 tablespoons self-raising flour, ⅓ cup (40g) coarsely chopped roasted pecans, 1 tablespoon brown sugar and 20g (¾oz) chopped butter in a small bowl; using fingertips, rub the mixture together until combined. Place pears cut-side up onto a baking-paper-lined oven tray; top pears with pecan crumble mixture. Bake about 15 minutes or until crumble is golden. Meanwhile, combine 1 cup (250ml) vanilla pouring custard, 2 tablespoons calvados (apple brandy) and a pinch ground cinnamon in a small saucpepan; cook, stirring, without boiling until heated through. Serve pears with custard.

tip You can use brandy or sherry instead of the calvados.

Choc-cranberry
BREAD PUDDINGS
PREP & COOK TIME 30 MINUTES
SERVES 4

Preheat oven to 160°C/325°F. Grease four 1½-cup (375ml) ovenproof dishes. Discard crusts from 8 slices white bread (320g). Spread slices with 50g (1½oz) softened butter; cut each slice into four triangles. Layer bread, overlapping, in dishes; sprinkle with 100g (3oz) coarsely chopped dark chocolate and ½ cup (65g) dried cranberries. Pour 1 litre (4 cups) thick vanilla custard over bread; sprinkle with a pinch ground nutmeg. Bake puddings about 20 minutes or until set (puddings will have a slight wobble in centre). Stand puddings 5 minutes before serving dusted with sifted icing (confectioners') sugar or cocoa powder.

Marmalade
CRÈME BRULÉE TARTS
PREP & COOK TIME 30 MINUTES
MAKES 8

Place eight 7cm (2¾-in) ready-made shortcrust pastry tartlet cases (150g) on an oven tray. Drop 1 teaspoon orange marmalade into each tartlet case. Divide ⅓ cup (80ml) thick vanilla custard into tartlet cases; tap gently to level surface. Sprinkle 2 tablespoons caster (superfine) sugar over custard. Using a blowtorch, caramelise sugar. Stand 5 minutes or until caramel cools and sets before serving.

tip You can use any marmalade or jam you like.

Glossary

ALLSPICE also known as pimento or jamaican pepper; so-named because it tastes like a combination of nutmeg, cumin, clove and cinnamon. Available whole (a dark-brown berry the size of a pea) or ground.

ALMONDS flat, pointy-tipped nuts with a pitted brown shell enclosing a creamy white kernel which is covered by a brown skin.
flaked paper-thin slices.
ground also called almond meal; nuts are powdered to a coarse flour-like texture.
slivered small pieces cut lengthways.

ARTICHOKE HEARTS tender centre of the globe artichoke; purchased, in brine, canned or in glass jars.

BAMBOO SHOOTS the tender shoots of bamboo plants, available in cans; must be rinsed and drained before use.

BASIL an aromatic herb; there are many types, but the most commonly used is sweet, or common, basil.

BEANS
green also known as french or string beans (although the tough string they once had has generally been bred out of them), this long thin fresh bean is consumed in its entirety once cooked.
kidney medium-size red bean, slightly floury in texture yet sweet in flavour; sold dried or canned, it's found in bean mixes and is used in chilli con carne.
sprouts also known as bean shoots; tender new growths of assorted beans and seeds germinated for consumption.
white a generic term we use for canned or dried cannellini, haricot, navy or great northern beans belonging to the same family, phaseolus vulgaris.

BREADCRUMBS
packaged fine-textured, crunchy, purchased white breadcrumbs.
panko also known as japanese breadcrumbs. They are available in two types: larger pieces and fine crumbs. Both have a lighter texture than Western-style breadcrumbs. They are available from Asian grocery stores and larger supermarkets.

BUK CHOY also known as buk choy, pak choi, chinese white cabbage or chinese chard; has a fresh, mild mustard taste. Use both stems and leaves. Baby buk choy, also known as pak kat farang or shanghai buk choy, is smaller and more tender than buk choy.

BUTTER use salted or unsalted (sweet) butter; 125g is equal to one stick of butter (4 ounces).

BUTTERMILK originally the term given to the slightly sour liquid left after butter was churned from cream, today it is made from no-fat or low-fat milk to which specific bacterial cultures have neen added. Despite its name, it is actually low in fat.

CAPSICUM (BELL PEPPER) also called pepper. Comes in many colours: red, green, yellow, orange and purplish-black. Be sure to discard seeds and membranes before use.

CAPERS grey-green buds of a warm climate shrub (usually Mediterranean); sold dried and salted or pickled in a vinegar brine. Baby capers are very small and have a fuller flavour. Rinse well before using.

CARAWAY SEEDS the small, half-moon-shaped dried seed from a member of the parsley family; adds a sharp anise flavour when used in both sweet and savoury dishes.

CARDAMOM a spice native to India and used extensively in its cuisine; can be purchased in pod, seed or ground form. Has a distinctive aromatic, sweetly rich flavour.

CAVOLO NERO or tuscan cabbage, a staple in Tuscan country cooking. It has long, narrow, wrinkled leaves and a rich and astringent, mild cabbage flavour. It doesn't lose its volume like silver beet or spinach when cooked, but it does need longer cooking.

CELERIAC (CELERY ROOT) tuberous root with knobbly brown skin, white flesh and a celery-like flavour.

CHEESE
blue these mould-treated cheeses are mottled with blue veining. Varieties include firm and crumbly stilton types to mild, creamy brie-like cheeses.
bocconcini walnut-sized, baby mozzarella, a delicate, semi-soft, white cheese traditionally made from buffalo milk. Sold fresh, it spoils rapidly so will only keep, refrigerated in brine, for 1 or 2 days at the most
fetta Greek in origin; a crumbly textured goat- or sheep-milk cheese having a sharp, salty taste. Ripened and stored in salted whey; particularly good cubed and tossed into salads.
goats made from goat milk, has an earthy, strong taste. Available in soft, crumbly and firm textures, in various shapes and sizes, and sometimes rolled in ash or herbs.
gorgonzola a creamy blue cheese having a mild, sweet taste.
labne is a soft cheese made by salting plain (natural) yoghurt and draining it of whey for up to 2 days until it becomes thick enough to roll into small balls, which may be sprinkled with or rolled in chopped herbs or spices.
mozzarella soft, spun-curd cheese; originating in southern Italy where it was traditionally made from water-buffalo milk.
parmesan also called parmigiano; is a hard, grainy cow-milk cheese originating in the Parma region of Italy.
pecorino the Italian generic name for cheeses made from sheep milk. If you can't find it, use parmesan.
pizza a blend of grated mozzarella, cheddar and parmesan cheeses.
ricotta a soft, sweet, moist, white cow-milk cheese with a low fat content (8.5%) and a slightly grainy texture. The name roughly translates as "cooked again" and refers to ricotta's manufacture from a whey that is itself a by-product of other cheese making.

CHERVIL also known as cicily; mildly fennel-flavoured member of the parsley family with curly dark-green leaves. Available both fresh and dried but, like all herbs, is best used fresh.

CHILLI generally, the smaller the chilli, the hotter it is. Use rubber gloves when seeding and chopping fresh chillies as they can burn your skin. Removing seeds and membranes lessens the heat level.
cayenne pepper a long, thin-fleshed, extremely hot red chilli usually sold dried and ground.

flakes also sold as crushed chilli; dehydrated deep-red extremely fine slices and whole seeds.

long available both fresh and dried; a generic term used for any moderately hot, long (6cm-8cm), thin chilli.

red thai a small, hot, bright red chilli.

sauce, sweet comparatively mild, fairly sticky and runny bottled sauce made from red chillies, sugar, garlic and white vinegar; used in Thai cooking.

CHINESE BARBECUED PORK also called char siew. Has a sweet-sticky coating made from soy sauce, sherry, five-spice powder and hoisin sauce. Available from Asian food stores.

CHORIZO a sausage of Spanish origin; made of coarsely ground pork and highly seasoned with garlic and chilli. They are deeply smoked, very spicy, and are available dry-cured or raw (which needs cooking).

CINNAMON available in pieces (called sticks or quills) and ground into powder; one of the world's most common spices, used as a sweet, fragrant flavouring for both sweet and savoury foods.

CLOVES dried flower buds of a tropical tree; can be used whole or in ground form. They have a strong scent and taste so should be used sparingly.

COCOA POWDER also known as unsweetened cocoa; cocoa beans (cacao seeds) that have been fermented, roasted, shelled, ground into powder then cleared of most of the fat content.

COCONUT

cream obtained commercially from the first pressing of the coconut flesh alone, without the addition of water; the second pressing (less rich) is sold as coconut milk. Available in cans and cartons at most supermarkets.

flaked dried flaked coconut flesh.

milk not the liquid found inside the fruit, which is called coconut water, but the diluted liquid from the second pressing of the white flesh of a mature coconut (the first pressing produces coconut cream). Available in cans and cartons at most supermarkets.

shredded unsweetened thin strips of dried coconut flesh.

sugar is not made from coconuts, but from the sap of the blossoms of the coconut palm tree. The refined sap looks a little like raw or light brown sugar, and has a similar caramel flavour. It also has the same amount of kilojoules as regular table (white) sugar.

CORIANDER also known as pak chee, cilantro or chinese parsley; a bright-green leafy herb with a pungent flavour. Both stems and roots of coriander are also used in cooking; wash well before using. Also available ground or as seeds; these should not be substituted for fresh coriander as the tastes are completely different.

CORNFLOUR (CORNSTARCH) available made from corn or wheat (wheaten cornflour gives a lighter texture in cakes); used as a thickening agent in cooking.

CREAM

pouring also called pure or fresh cream. It contains no additives and has a minimum fat content of 35%.

sour a thick cultured soured cream. Minimum fat content of 35%.

thick (double) a dolloping cream with a minimum fat content of 45%.

thickened (heavy) a whipping cream that contains a thickener. It has a minimum fat content of 35%.

CURRY

green paste the hottest of the traditional pastes; contains chilli, garlic, onion, salt, lemon grass, spices and galangal.

tandoori paste a highly-seasoned classic East-Indian marinade flavoured with garlic, tamarind, ginger, coriander, chilli and other spices, and used to give foods the authentic red-orange tint of tandoor oven cooking.

red a popular curry paste; a hot blend of red chilli, garlic, shallot, lemon grass, salt, galangal, shrimp paste, kaffir lime peel, coriander, cumin and paprika. It is milder than the hotter thai green curry paste.

tom yum paste a Thai-style paste with a hot, spicy and sour flavour. Containing lemon grass, red chilli, sugar, onion, anchovy, galangal, kaffir lime and paprika. It is used to make the traditional spicy sour prawn soup known as tom yum goong.

yellow one of the mildest Thai pastes; it is similar in appearance to Indian curries as they both include yellow chilli and fresh turmeric. Good blended with coconut in vegetable, rice and noodle dishes.

EGGPLANT also known as aubergine.

FENNEL also called finocchio or anise; a crunchy green vegetable slightly resembling celery that's eaten raw in salads; fried as an accompaniment; or used as an ingredient in soups and sauces. Also the name given to the dried seeds of the plant which have a stronger licorice flavour.

FENUGREEK a member of the pea family, the seeds have a bitter taste; the ground seeds are used in Indian curries, powders and pastes.

FILLO PASTRY paper-thin sheets of raw pastry; brush each sheet with oil or melted butter, stack in layers, then cut and fold as directed.

FLOUR

plain (all-purpose) a general all-purpose wheat flour.

self-raising plain flour sifted with baking powder in the proportion of 1 cup flour to 2 teaspoons baking powder.

GAI LAN also known as chinese broccoli, gai larn, kanah, gai lum and chinese kale; appreciated more for its stems than its coarse leaves.

GARAM MASALA a blend of spices including cardamom, cinnamon, cloves, coriander, fennel and cumin, roasted and ground together. Black pepper and chilli can be added for a hotter version.

GHEE clarified butter; with the milk solids removed, this fat has a high smoking point so can be heated to a high temperature without burning. Used as a cooking medium in Indian recipes.

GINGER

fresh also called green or root ginger; the thick gnarled root of a tropical plant.

ground also called powdered ginger; used as a flavouring in baking but cannot be substituted for fresh ginger.

GOW GEE WRAPPERS made of flour, egg and water, are found in the refrigerated or freezer section of Asian food shops and many supermarkets. These come in different thicknesses and shapes.

KAFFIR LIME LEAVES also known as bai magrood. Aromatic leaves of a citrus tree; two glossy dark green leaves joined end to end, forming a rounded hourglass shape. A strip of fresh lime peel may be substituted for each kaffir lime leaf.

KUMARA the Polynesian name of an orange-fleshed sweet potato often confused with yam.

LAMB'S TONGUE also called lamb's lettuce, mâche and corn salad, has small, tender, velvety leaves. It is sold in punnets and is available from autumn into spring.

LEMON GRASS a tall, clumping, lemon-smelling and -tasting, sharp-edged grass; the white part of the stem is used, finely chopped, in cooking.

MAPLE SYRUP also called pure maple syrup; distilled from the sap of sugar maple trees found only in Canada and the USA. Maple-flavoured syrup or pancake syrup is not an adequate substitute for the real thing.

MIXED SPICE a classic spice mixture generally containing caraway, allspice, coriander, cumin, nutmeg and ginger, although cinnamon and other spices can be added. It is used with fruit and in cakes.

MUSHROOMS

portobello are mature, fully opened swiss browns; they are larger and bigger in flavour.

shiitake when fresh are also known as chinese black, forest or golden oak mushrooms; although cultivated, they are large and meaty and have the earthiness and taste of wild mushrooms. When dried, they are known as donko or dried chinese mushrooms; rehydrate before use.

swiss brown also known as cremini or roman mushrooms; are light brown mushrooms with a full-bodied flavour.

MUSTARD

dijon pale brown, distinctively flavoured, mild-tasting french mustard.

wholegrain also known as seeded mustard. A French-style coarse-grain mustard made from crushed mustard seeds and Dijon-style french mustard.

MUSTARD SEEDS are available in black, brown or yellow varieties. Available from major supermarkets and health-food shops.

NOODLES

dried rice stick see rice vermicelli, dried (below).

rice vermicelli dried very fine noodles made from rice flour and water, vermicelli is often compressed into blocks and dried. Before using, soak in boiling water until tender.

ONIONS

green also known as scallion or, incorrectly, shallot; an immature onion picked before the bulb has formed. Has a long, bright-green edible stalk.

red also known as spanish, red spanish or bermuda onion; a sweet-flavoured, large, purple-red onion.

shallots also called french shallots, golden shallots or eschalots; small, brown-skinned, elongated members of the onion family.

spring have small white bulbs and long, narrow, green-leafed tops.

PAPRIKA ground, dried, sweet red capsicum (bell pepper); there are many types available, including sweet, hot, mild and smoked.

POLENTA also known as cornmeal; a flour-like cereal made of ground corn (maize). Also the name of the dish made from it.

SAUCES

fish also called nam pla or nuoc nam; made from pulverised salted fermented fish, most often anchovies. Has a pungent smell and strong taste, so use sparingly.

plum a thick, sweet and sour dipping sauce made from plums, vinegar, sugar, chillies and spices.

soy made from fermented soya beans. Several variations are available in most supermarkets and Asian food stores.

dark soy deep brown, almost black in colour; rich, with a thicker consistency than other types. Pungent but not that salty.

SILVER BEET also known as swiss chard; mistakenly called spinach.

SUGAR

brown very soft, finely granulated sugar retaining molasses for its characteristic colour and flavour.

caster also known as superfine or finely granulated table sugar.

palm also known as nam tan pip, jaggery, jawa or gula melaka; made from the sap of the sugar palm tree. Light brown to black in colour and usually sold in rock-hard cakes. Substitute with brown sugar if unavailable.

SUGAR SNAP PEAS also known as honey snap peas; fresh small peas that can be eaten whole, pod and all, similarly to snow peas.

SUMAC a purple-red, astringent spice ground from berries growing on shrubs that flourish wild around the Mediterranean; has a tart, lemony flavour

TAMARIND PASTE the distillation of tamarind pulp into a condensed compacted paste with a sweet-sour, slightly astringent taste. Thick and purple-black, it requires no soaking. Found in Asian food stores.

TURMERIC related to ginger; adds a golden-yellow colour to food.

VINEGAR

red wine based on fermented red wine.

white wine made from white wine.

VIETNAMESE MINT not a mint at all, but a pungent and peppery narrow-leafed member of the buckwheat family.

WATERCRESS one of the cress family, a large group of peppery greens. Highly perishable, so must be used as soon as possible after purchase. It has an exceptionally high vitamin K content.

YOGHURT, GREEK-STYLE plain yoghurt that has been strained in a cloth (muslin) to remove the whey and to give it a creamy consistency.

ZUCCHINI also called courgette; small, pale- or dark-green or yellow vegetable of the squash family.

Conversion chart

Measures

One Australian metric measuring cup holds approximately 250ml; one Australian metric tablespoon holds 20ml; one Australian metric teaspoon holds 5ml.

The difference between one country's measuring cups and another's is within a two- or three-teaspoon variance, and will not affect your cooking results.
North America, New Zealand and the United Kingdom use a 15ml tablespoon.

All cup and spoon measurements are level. The most accurate way of measuring dry ingredients is to weigh them. When measuring liquids, use a clear glass or plastic jug with the metric markings.

The imperial measurements used in these recipes are approximate only. Measurements for cake pans are approximate only. Using same-shaped cake pans of a similar size should not affect the outcome of your baking. We measure the inside top of the cake pan to determine sizes.

We use large eggs with an average weight of 60g.

Dry measures

METRIC	IMPERIAL
15G	½OZ
30G	1OZ
60G	2OZ
90G	3OZ
125G	4OZ (¼LB)
155G	5OZ
185G	6OZ
220G	7OZ
250G	8OZ (½LB)
280G	9OZ
315G	10OZ
345G	11OZ
375G	12OZ (¾LB)
410G	13OZ
440G	14OZ
470G	15OZ
500G	16OZ (1LB)
750G	24OZ (1½LB)
1KG	32OZ (2LB)

Liquid measures

METRIC	IMPERIAL
30ML	1 FLUID OZ
60ML	2 FLUID OZ
100ML	3 FLUID OZ
125ML	4 FLUID OZ
150ML	5 FLUID OZ
190ML	6 FLUID OZ
250ML	8 FLUID OZ
300ML	10 FLUID OZ
500ML	16 FLUID OZ
600ML	20 FLUID OZ
1000ML (1 LITRE)	1¾ PINTS

Length measures

METRIC	IMPERIAL
3MM	⅛IN
6MM	¼IN
1CM	½IN
2CM	¾IN
2.5CM	1IN
5CM	2IN
6CM	2½IN
8CM	3IN
10CM	4IN
13CM	5IN
15CM	6IN
18CM	7IN
20CM	8IN
22CM	9IN
25CM	10IN
28CM	11IN
30CM	12IN (1FT)

Oven temperatures

The oven temperatures in this book are for conventional ovens; if you have a fan-forced oven, decrease the temperature by 10-20 degrees.

	°C (CELSIUS)	°F (FAHRENHEIT)
VERY SLOW	120	250
SLOW	150	300
MODERATELY SLOW	160	325
MODERATE	180	350
MODERATELY HOT	200	400
HOT	220	425
VERY HOT	240	475

Index